Teacher's Edition

Phonics is Fun

Book 2

By Louis Krane, Ed. D.

Reprinted and electronically reproduced by permission of Pearson Education, Inc., New York, NY.

Copyright 2017 by St. Jerome Homeschool Library Press

Original copyright 1990 by Pearson Education, Inc., publishing as Modern Curriculum Press

STJEROMEHOMESCHOOLLIBRARY.ORG

St. Jerome Homeschool Library & Bookstore

A Nonprofit for Affordable Home Education

All rights reserved. No part of this book may be reproduced or transmitted in any form or by any means, electronic

or mechanical, including photocopying, recording, or by any information storage or retrieval system,

without written permission from the publisher.

Phonics Is Fun

Faster-paced instruction for more capable students.
Now, from MCP, a phonics program that maximizes students' ability to learn
as it minimizes teacher-preparation time.

Complete, systematic phonics instruction

Phonics Is Fun provides instruction in the minimum number of phonetic skills which will assure word recognition. The sequence of these essential skills is based on the frequency with which phonetic elements occur in the English language. Thus, the scope and sequence of skills is designed to provide students with a viable set of phonetic word-attack skills, enabling them to read an unlimited number of words.

More capable students quickly take responsibility for their own learning

The instruction is accomplished through a multi-sensory approach, using auditory and visual discrimination exercises, sound blending, and word pronunciation, and culminating in reading, spelling, and writing words in sentences. The students are presented with the minimum number of rules and definitions for achieving reading independence. The students quickly develop the ability to relate the printed word to its speech equivalent and comprehend the meaning of words in context.

All new, contemporary artwork

The attractive, clear artwork will hold students' interest as they work through the pages. The picture cues provide for vocabulary development, but since they are easy to identify, they never interfere with the learning of the phonetic skills.

New, expanded Teacher's Edition

This Teacher's Edition maximizes your teaching efforts as it minimizes the amount of preparation time. There is an array of completely described games and activities for multisensory practice of phonetic skills. These games and activities only require common, easily found materials. The pictures are clearly labeled and the answers easily readable. Blackline masters provide for skills assessment, and family involvement activities enable you to keep parents informed of their children's progress.

Student Edition with instruction that moves at a faster, more challenging pace.

More items per page, providing more concentrated practice.

Faster, more challenging pace of instruction.

Variety of formats to hold students' attention.

All-new, interest-capturing artwork.

Students master the minimum number of important phonetic skills, applying them in meaningful contexts.

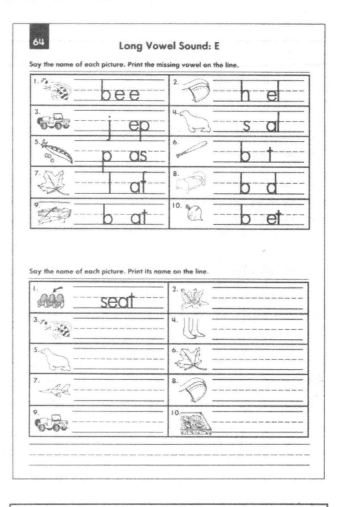

Teacher's Edition that maximizes your time.

Review automatically builds in maintenance of previously-learned phonetic skills.

Teaching Ideas describes games and activities that provide multisensory involvement through listening, speaking, reading and writing.

Reteaching suggests activities for helping students who didn't master the skill the first time through.

Extension challenges students who have been successful.

Blackline masters for assessment.

Family Involvement activities that are cross-referenced with reproducible letters to parents.

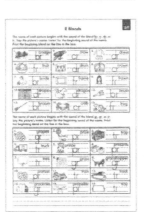

Scope and Sequence for Phonics Is Fun

Lesson Numbers

Skill	Book 1	Book 2	Book 3
Visual Discrimination	1		
Recognition of Letters	2–7	1	1
Consonant Letter-Sound Associations	8–27	2–10	2–4
Short Vowels: A	28–30	11	5
I	31–33	12	6
U	34–36	13	7
O	37–39	14	8
E	40–42	15	9
Long Vowels: A	43–45	18	11
I	46–48	19	11
U	49–51	20	12
O	52–54	21	12
E	55–57	22	13
Review of Vowels 58			
Suffixes	59–61	36–45	39–44, 57
Consonant Blends: R Blends	62	24	15
L Blends	63	25	16
S Blends	64	26	17
Y as a Vowel	65	27	20
Consonant Digraphs	66–68	29, 30, 58, 59	18, 19, 34, 35
Compound Words	16, 23	10,14	
Two-Syllable Words		17, 23	10
W as a Vowel		28	20
Hard and Soft C and G		31, 32	21–23
Vowels with R		33–35	24–26
Contractions		46–49	58
Vowel Digraphs	50–53	27–30	
Kn		58	35
Wr		59	35
Ending Le		60	36
Prefixes		61	46–49
Synonyms		62	59
Antonyms		63	60
Homonyms		64	61
Diphthongs		54–57	31–33
Syllabication			37, 38, 45, 50–56

To the Teacher

The *Phonics Is Fun* program consists of a phonetic-semantic approach to word recognition. Characterized by strong auditory training, the program presents a minimum of rules, definitions, and variations of consonant and vowel sounds. In *Phonics Is Fun*, the child quickly develops the ability to associate letters and sounds, relate the printed word to its speech equivalent, and comprehend the meaning of words in context. The program increases the child's reading vocabulary to correspond with the verbal and auditory vocabulary. *Phonics Is Fun* is designed to provide the child with a viable set of phonetic decoding skills, enabling the reading of an unlimited number of words.

Objective of the Program

The specific objective of the *Phonics Is Fun* program is to provide for mastery of the minimum number of phonetic skills that will assure achievement in word recognition. The sequence in which these skills are developed is based on the frequency with which phonetic elements occur in the English language.

Instruction is accomplished through a multisensory approach. Activities include auditory, visual, and tactile discrimination exercises, as well as sound blending, word pronunciation, reading, spelling, and writing words within the context of sentences.

Characteristics of the Program

The focus of *Phonics Is Fun* is not memorization of phonetic axioms. Instead, the emphasis is for the child to identify elements the phonetic principles address, state rules in personal language, and apply each rule, tip, and definition to appropriate words.

Phonics Is Fun, Book 1, presents the recognition of the letters of the alphabet, single consonants, short and long vowels, *Y* as a vowel, consonant blends, consonant digraphs, and endings *-s, -ed*, and *-ing*.

Phonics Is Fun, Book 2, reviews and extends the skills taught in *Book 1*. It also introduces hard and soft *C* and *G*, *W* as a vowel, vowel digraphs, vowels with *R*, affixes, contractions, synonyms, antonyms, and homonyms.

Phonics Is Fun, Book 3, reviews and broadens the skills taught in *Book 1* and *Book 2* prior to presenting syllabication.

The acquisition of phonetic skills is cumulative in nature, with subsequent levels of instruction building on prior teaching. The following phonetic rules are developed in *Books 1* and *2* of *Phonics Is Fun*, then are expanded upon in *Book 3: Short Vowel Rule, Long Vowel Rule 1, Long Vowel Rule 2, Y as a Consonant, Y as Long I, Y as Long E, Vowel W Rule, Soft C Rule*, and *Soft G Rule*. Rules, tips, and definitions are explicitly defined in appropriate lessons in the Teacher's Manual.

Implementing the Program

This Teacher's Edition presents lesson plans that can be used effectively with an individual child, a small group, or an entire class. Each activity is designated with a boldface title to be easily located. You can choose activities based on time considerations, availability of materials, and academic needs. (For instance, you might conduct the activities in some lessons over the span of two class sessions.) Recommended materials are common to most classrooms. Preparation options are suggested when appropriate, and an effort has been made to include the children in these preparations.

The lesson plans contain the following sections: Assessment, Review, Teaching Ideas, Reteaching, and Extension. The first lesson in each book will begin with an Assessment activity. A Review section appears only when the reteaching of an earlier skill will help the child grasp the new concept presented in the Teaching Ideas section. Skills are developed in Teaching Ideas, redeveloped in Reteaching, and enriched in Extension. While the activities in Teaching Ideas are intended for implementation with the entire class, the Reteaching and Extension exercises are directed to the individual child. Reduced facsimiles of Pupil Edition pages appear on the same page as the corresponding lesson to insure that specific practice follows immediately after instruction.

Involving the Family

Family Involvement Letters are referenced in most teaching units and are provided at the back of each Teacher's Edition for duplication. The activities suggested in these letters are designed to acquaint families with the work their child is doing in *Phonics Is Fun*, and to provide further review and reinforcement of the skills. Families choosing to participate in these activities will find each activity presented in a step-by-step format, with materials that involve little preparation and are common to most homes. While participation in these activities is not mandatory, the teacher may choose to use submitted projects as part of the classroom display or materials.

Contents

Lesson 1
The Alphabet *A* Through *Z* (pages 1–2)

Objective   The child will identify the letters *A* through *Z* in isolation and in mixed order.

Assessment

Listening   To practice rhyming skills, read aloud the following sentences, asking volunteers to name the two rhyming words in each.

1. I saw a frog hop on a log.
2. The kitten sat on Daddy's hat.
3. April showers bring May flowers.
4. We like to play on a summer day.
5. The happy pig danced a jig.
6. Can a fish make a wish?

Teaching Ideas

Speaking   Ask for a volunteer to distribute the letter cards *A* through *Z*, small and capital. Invite the child holding capital *A* to place it on the chalkboard ledge and say the letter name. Then, ask the child holding small *a* to place it next to its partner letter and say, "This is small *a*." Continue in this manner throughout the entire alphabet.

Write the following words on the chalkboard and ask for volunteers to name the letters in each word in left-to-right progression.

cat	*vine*	*him*	*rod*	*quiz*
dip	*zip*	*past*	*feel*	*you*
no	*bug*	*wax*	*Jane*	*kitchen*

Writing   You might dictate the spelling of the following words for the children, as they write the words on their papers: *desk, vine, flag, coat, sip, quit, any, hot, wax, bun, jet, zoo.*

Extension

Partner-Letter Game   Arrange the capital letter alphabet cards in random order faceup on a table. Place the corresponding small letters facedown in a pile. Invite the child to draw a small letter card and place it on top of its partner letter. Provide encouragement if the child should confuse *B* and *D*, for example, by pointing out the differences between those letters.

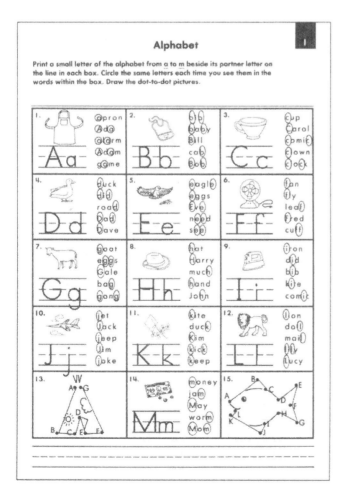

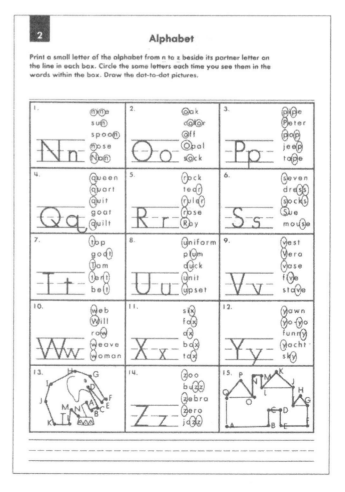

Unit 2 Consonants

Lesson 2
Consonant Sounds *S* and *T* (pages 3–4)

Objective   The child will associate the letters *S* and *T* with their respective sounds.

Review

Speaking   To review the letters of the alphabet, show the letter cards, capital and small, in mixed order. Ask the children to name the letter on each card.

Teaching Ideas

Listening   Say the following words that begin with the letters *S* and *T*. Ask the children to name the consonant heard at the beginning of each word: *turkey, squirrel, tickle, sail, turtle, tomatoes, seven, silly, soft.*

Say the following words, and have the children name the beginning and the ending consonant heard in each word: *sit, spiders, tapes, toys, scissors, suit, tent, tigers, toot.*

Writing   Select eight or ten picture flashcards containing objects with names that begin and end with *S* or *T*. Arrange the picture flashcards in view of the children. Draw on the chalkboard, above each picture flashcard, a split box like the following.

Invite volunteers to name each picture and print the beginning and ending sounds of each name in the split box.

You may wish to have the children print the following sentences on strips of paper. Place the strips in an empty box.

1. *My toes hurt.*
2. *Tony sat on the sand.*
3. *The eggs rolled off the table.*
4. *Six toads ran under the tent.*
5. *Two cats were on the seat.*
6. *The bus stops here.*

Invite each volunteer to draw a sentence strip out of the box. Ask the children to read their sentences aloud, identifying the words containing the *S* and *T* sounds. You may want to have volunteers write these words on the chalkboard.

Extension

Art   Invite the child to draw a picture of a snake and a picture of a turtle on separate sheets of paper. Ask the child to identify the sound heard at the beginning of each word. Have the child put a large *S* and a large *T* above the appropriate drawing. Give the child an assortment of picture flashcards containing objects with names that begin with *S* or *T*. Invite the child to name each object and then place the picture flashcard on the drawing that has a name that begins with the same sound.

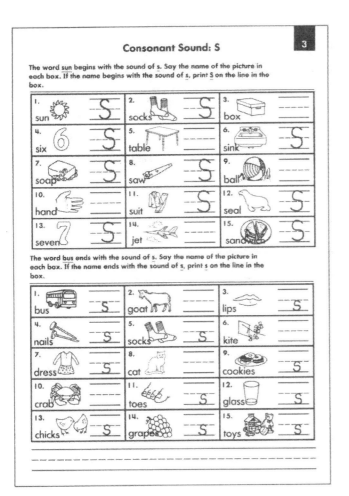

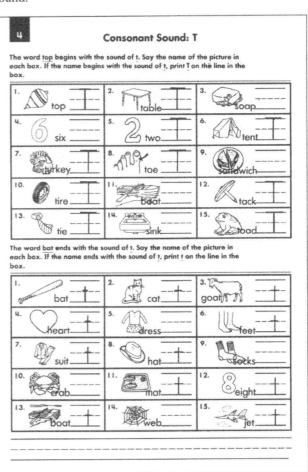

11

Lesson 3
Consonant Sound *B* (pages 5–6)

Objective   The child will identify the name and sound of the letter *B*.

Review

Zoo Game   To review the consonant sounds of *S* and *T*, play the Zoo Game. Hold up the letter card for *S* and say, *I am going to visit a seal and I will take a sled with me.* Ask a volunteer to "visit" the seal, taking along a sled plus one other object that begins with the *S* sound. Have each subsequent volunteer suggest a new *S* object to bring in addition to the sled. When the children have exhausted their supply of words beginning with *S*, shift to visiting a tiger and bringing along objects with names beginning with *T*.

Teaching Ideas

Speaking   You may wish to say the following words and ask the children to name the beginning sound in each word: *banana, bird, bug, belt, bus, boys, bent, bat, boat.*

Then, write the following words on the chalkboard: *bib, bait, boat, scrub, beads, bat, beans, but, bent.*

Invite volunteers to read a word and identify *B* as the beginning or ending sound.

Hot-Potato-Letters Game   Distribute eight or ten picture flashcards containing objects, some of which have names that begin or end with the letter *B*. Explain that the children will be playing a variation of the Hot-Potato Game.

Invite the children to sit in a circle. Play music while the children pass the picture flashcards to the left. Stop the music after an appropriate interval, asking the children who are holding picture flashcards with an object name that begins or ends with the letter *B* to stand. Invite these children to say the name of the object on their picture flashcards. Then collect these picture flashcards, and ask them to rejoin the circle. Redistribute the picture flashcards and repeat the round. Continue until most of the children have had a turn. After several repetitions, you may wish to designate another beginning or ending sound, such as *S* or *T*, as the "Hot Potato."

Extension

Reading   Write the following sentences on the chalkboard.
1. *The bear likes the red ball.*
2. *The baby has seven toys.*
3. *Brian is bumping the table.*
4. *The boats sail in the lake.*
5. *Sam takes the book.*

Ask the child to read each sentence and identify the words containing the letters *S, T,* and *B*.

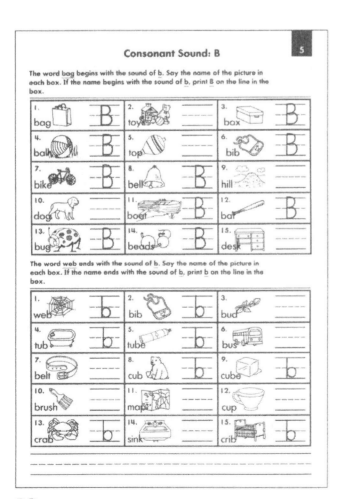

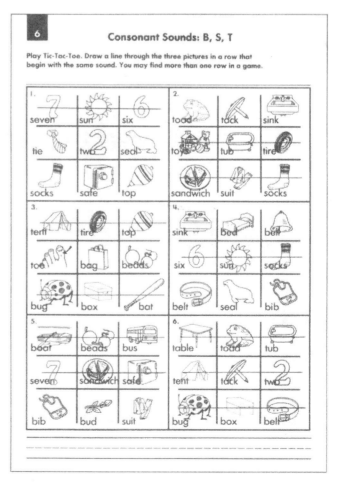

12

Lesson 4
Consonant Sounds *H, J,* and *M*   (pages 7–8)

Objective   The child will associate the letters *H, J,* and *M* with their respective sounds.

Review

Riddle Game   To review rhyming skills and the consonant sounds of *S, T,* and *B,* challenge the children with riddles using the following picture flashcards: *sun, boat, bed, box, top.* Display the picture flashcards on the chalkboard ledge. Then ask the children to identify the appropriate pictures.

1. It rhymes with pop *and begins with* T.
2. It rhymes with bun *and begins with* S.
3. It rhymes with fox *and begins with* B.
4. It rhymes with coat *and begins with* B.
5. It rhymes with red *and begins with* B.

Teaching Ideas

Listening   Challenge the children by saying the following words and inviting them to identify the beginning sound in each: *milk, house, jelly, hide, jeep, him, mother, joke, Martin.* Write the beginning consonants on the chalkboard as the children identify the sounds they make. Point to each consonant, name it, and ask the children to repeat the consonant sound. Encourage volunteers to trace the consonants on the chalkboard.

Speaking   Invite the children to name the words that begin with the targeted consonants for each of the following sentences.

1. J: John played a joke on Jamil.
2. H: Hannah hit a home run today.
3. M: Mr. Mills likes to eat meat.
4. H: Dad has a hammer at home.
5. M: Mara has many marvelous marbles.
6. J: Jim put a jelly bean in a jar.

Reteaching

Writing   You might wish to write the following words on the chalkboard and underline the consonants *H, J,* and *M* wherever they appear: *Mom, hats, Jack, joke, Mike, jam, ham.* Encourage the child to use the words in sentences. Invite the child to try to use more than one of the words in each sentence.

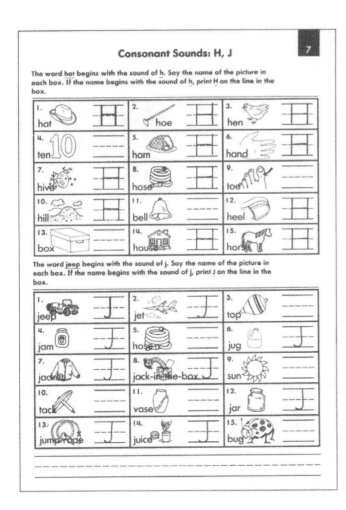

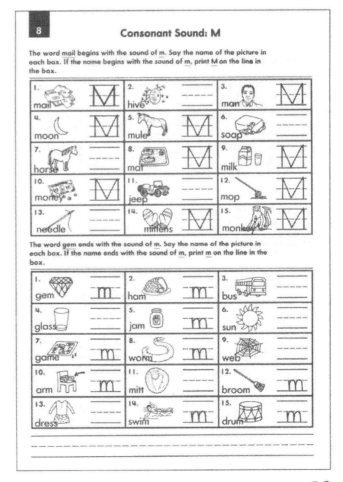

Lesson 5
Consonant Sound *K*   (pages 9–10)

Objective   The child will identify the name and the sound of the letter *K*.

Review

Listening   To practice the recognition of various consonant sounds, you may wish to display the letter cards for *S*, *T*, *B*, *H*, *J*, and *M*. Encourage the children to identify the beginning sounds of the words as you say them. Pronounce the following words, challenging the children to come to the front of the classroom and to point to the letter card that shows the beginning sound of each word: *sunshine, beads, honey, tulip, mirror, janitor, sausage, mouse, television, hush, jigsaw.*

Teaching Ideas

Listening   Say the following words and invite the children to identify the beginning sound in each: *kitchen, kind, kettle, king, kitten, keep.* Explain to the children that the beginning sound they hear is the sound of the letter *K.*

To continue the activity, say the following words and challenge the children to tell you whether the *K* sound is heard at the beginning or at the end of each word: *brick, park, thank, Chuck.*

Speaking   Write the following words on the chalkboard: *Kim, Jack, kite, jam, kit, kick, Mom, back, make, key, brick, black.* Invite volunteers to read each word and to identify the beginning and the ending sounds in each. Encourage the children to come forward and circle the letter *K* whenever it appears.

To extend the activity, challenge the children to create a sentence for each word that contains the letter *K.*

Hot-Potato-Letters Game   Invite the children to play the Hot-Potato-Letters Game introduced in Lesson 3 in this unit. Adapt the game for use with the letters *H, J, M,* and *K.*

Extension

Writing   Write the following words on the chalkboard and draw a split box above each word.

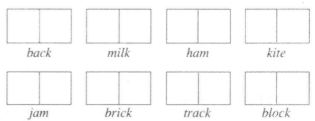

back	*milk*	*ham*	*kite*
jam	*brick*	*track*	*block*

Encourage the child to read each word aloud and to write the beginning sound and the ending sound in the appropriate half of the split box above each word.

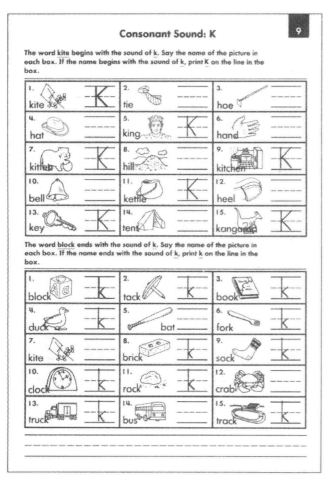

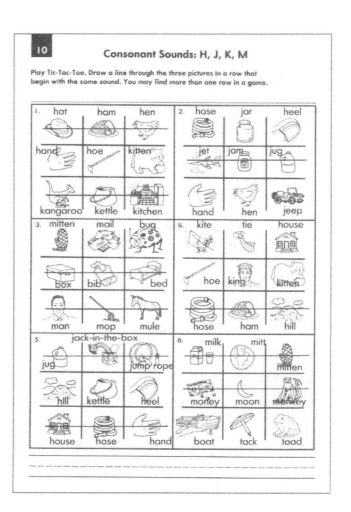

Lesson 6
Consonant Sounds *F* and *G* (pages 11–12)

Objective   The child will associate the letters *F* and *G* with their respective sounds.

Review

Riddle Game   To practice the consonant sounds of *H*, *J*, *M*, and *K*, you might wish to develop riddles using the following picture flashcards: *moon, house, kittens, jeep, key*. Play the Riddle Game, as described in Lesson 4 of this unit, using the following riddles.

    1. It shines in the sky and begins with M.
    2. You can live in one, and it begins with H.
    3. Mother cats have them, and they begin with K.
    4. People drive it, and it begins with J.
    5. It unlocks a door and begins with K.

Teaching Ideas

Listening   Say the following words and challenge the children to identify the beginning sound of each: *faucet, garden, goose, fiddle, free, garage, grapefruit, gum, fire, fly*. Point out the beginning *F* and *G* for the children as they identify them. Then write the letters on the chalkboard.

If you wish to extend the activity, say the following words and encourage the children to clap whenever they hear a word beginning with *G*: *goat, girl, king, get, kitten, game, flag, key, goose, kangaroo, gate*.

Speaking   Pronounce the following words: *four, muff, loaf, muffler, puff, funny, snowflake*. Challenge the children to repeat each word and to tell whether the sound of *F* is heard at the beginning, the middle, or the end of the word.

Extension

Writing   Write the following sentences on the chalkboard or duplicate them on paper for the children.

    1. The fish swam in the glass.
    2. The grass is green.
    3. The pig and the goat ate bugs.
    4. Fay will go to get five fans.
    5. We had fun with Fred's cats.
    6. Put fresh paint on the gate.

Direct the child to circle the words that contain the letter *F* and to underline the words that contain the letter *G*. You may wish to help the child write the circled and the underlined words in alphabetical order on a separate sheet of paper.

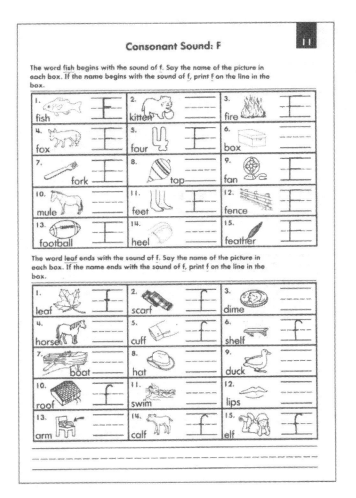

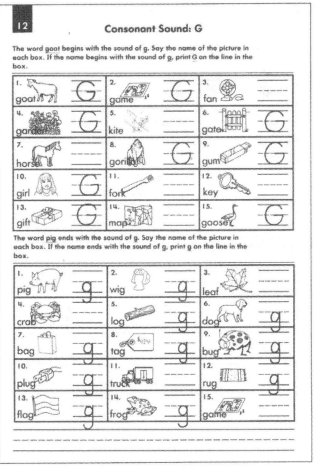

Lesson 7
Consonant Sounds *D* and *L*   (pages 13–15)

Objective   The child will associate the letters *D* and *L* with their respective sounds.

Review

Listening   To review auditory discrimination, pronounce words that begin or end with the sounds of *B, G, H, K, M, T,* or *S*. Words you might use include the following: *ghost, heart, jacks, bug, suit, kite, goat, mitt, bat, gas, hike.* After you have said each word, ask a volunteer to write the beginning and the ending consonant sound of each word on the chalkboard. Encourage children who give incorrect responses to repeat the word after you before attempting another guess.

Teaching Ideas

Listening   Write the letters *D* and *L* on the chalkboard, reviewing the sound of each. Then pronounce the following words beginning with the sounds of *D* and *L* and invite volunteers to identify the beginning sound of each word: *December, dog, lake, dentist, ladder, lion, daddy, lock, desk, laugh, dairy, donkey.*

Continue the activity by pronouncing words that end with one of the targeted sounds, such as the following: *Bill, sled, bread, said, toad, hill, ball, hide, doll.* Ask the children to identify the ending consonant sound in each word. You might write each word on the chalkboard to provide visual confirmation of the children's responses.

Name-Club Game   Ask the children to pretend there is a club for people whose names begin or end with the consonant sounds of either *D* or *L*. Invite volunteers to suggest names that members could have. To reinforce the lesson and to recognize children who give correct responses, record suggested names that qualify on the chalkboard. You might begin by identifying the names of children in the class that begin with *D* or *L*. These children may want to write their own names on the chalkboard.

Reading   Distribute the following word cards: *did, lid, doll, led, laid, lied, dig, luck, lost, sell, meal.* Have the children read the words and name the beginning and the ending consonant for each.

Write the following sentences on the chalkboard.
1. *Daddy will buy Dave a dog.*
2. *Did you sell your yellow duck to Luke?*
3. *Go up the hill and get my lamb.*
4. *The lazy lion likes to sleep.*

Ask a volunteer to read each sentence and to circle the words that contain the *D* and *L* consonants.

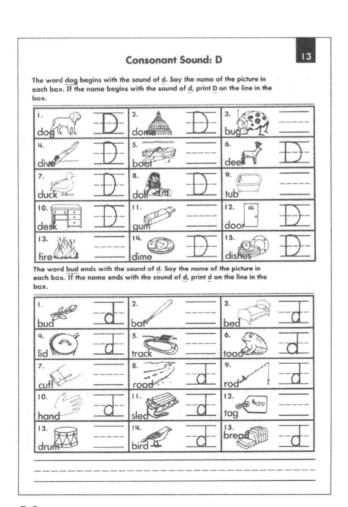

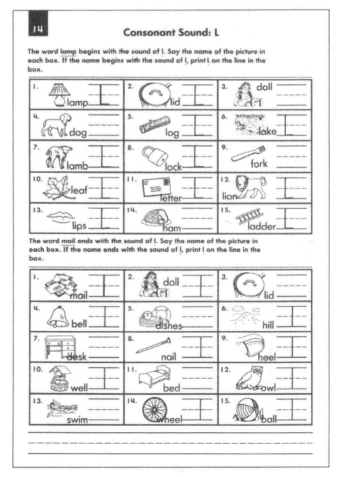

Develop an awareness of the targeted sounds by challenging the children to create questions based on the above sentences, such as the following.

1. Which sentences name animals that begin with D?

2. Which sentence uses the most words that begin with L?

Encourage the children to offer support for their answers.

Extension

Memory Game   Play the following variation of a classic memory game to develop both memory and phonics skills. Ask the child to complete the following sentence with a word that begins with either *D* or *L: I went on a trip and I took a _____* . Repeat the child's sentence, adding another item that begins with *D* or *L* that was taken on the trip. Challenge the child to repeat your sentence and to add an additional item to the sequence. Continue the game until the items are repeated out of sequence or an item is included that does not begin with either of the targeted letters.

Lesson 8
Consonant Sounds N, W, and C (pages 16–17)

Objective The child will associate the hard sound of *C* and the consonant sounds of *N* and *W* with their respective letters.

Review

Speaking To review beginning consonant sounds, challenge the children to name words that begin with the following letters: *S, T, B, H, M, J, K, F, G, D, L*. Reinforce correct responses by writing the words on the chalkboard and circling the targeted letters.

Teaching Ideas

Speaking Write the letters *N, W,* and *C* as column headings on the chalkboard and invite volunteers to say the consonant sound of each. Challenge the children to name at least three words that begin with each sound. Record the correct responses on the chalkboard under the appropriate letter.

Listening Remind the children that consonant sounds may be heard at the beginning, in the middle, or at the end of words. Ask one row of children to stand. Then read a list of words that contain the *N* consonant sound, such as: *night, pin, banner, new, winner.* Have each child repeat a word and tell where in the word (beginning, middle, or end) the targeted sound occurs. Continue the exercise with other rows of children, using the sounds of hard *C* and *W*. Suitable words include the following.

C: *cat, picnic, crocodile, cucumber, card, caterpillar*
W: *wiggle, tower, wolf, water, power, winter, well*

Mail-the-Letter Game To practice auditory discrimination of the consonant sounds, draw three boxes on the chalkboard. Label the boxes *N, W,* and *C*. Explain to the children that these are mailboxes and that each box can only take cards with words beginning with the letter shown on the box. Then distribute word cards containing the following words: *can, wag, wind, not, neck, went, cane, nine, weed, cat, cup, nose, nest.* Have each card read and then "mailed" by placing it on the chalkboard ledge beneath the mailbox showing the correct beginning consonant.

Reteaching

Research Have the child compile a list of the first names of the children in the class. Challenge the child to examine the completed list and to circle the names that have the consonant sounds of *N, W,* and *C*. If the child has difficulty, you may wish to provide a few names with the targeted sounds. (You may wish to save these lists for use in later lessons.)

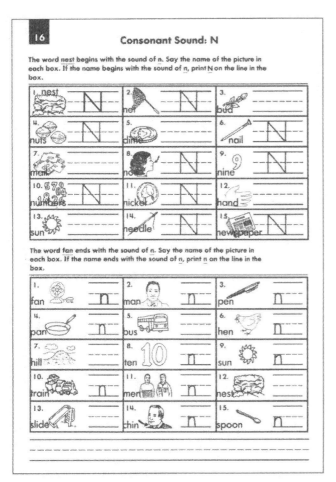

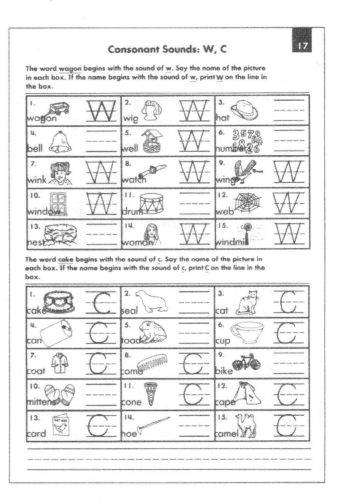

Lesson 9
Consonant Sounds *R* and *P*   (pages 18–20)

Objective   The child will associate the letters *R* and *P* with their respective sounds.

Review

Art   Ask for the children's help in creating picture flashcards for an auditory discrimination exercise. Give each child an unlined 3" x 5" card. On the card, have each child draw a picture of something that begins or ends with the letter *B, D, H, L, N, W, K,* or *S* or the hard consonant sound of *C* or *G.* On the back of each card, have the child write the name of the object and underline the targeted beginning or ending consonant sound. Invite each child to show a picture flashcard to the class. Have volunteers name each picture and identify the beginning and the ending sounds.

Teaching Ideas

Listening/Speaking   Write the letters *R* and *P* as column headings on the chalkboard. Ask a volunteer to say the consonant sound of each. Challenge the children to name at least three words that begin with each sound and to record correct responses under the appropriate headings. To provide practice with the targeted consonants as final sounds, write *car* and *door* under the *R* heading and *flap* and *mop* under the *P* heading. Have a volunteer point out the final consonant sound in each word. Then challenge that child to think of a rhyming word that ends with the same sound. You might ask other children to suggest additional rhyming words.

Writing   Write the following words on the chalkboard: *fed, lock, tin, wig, sing, hope, mail, fan, take, ten, ripe, jet.* Ask a child to read a word and to change the beginning consonant by writing either *P* or *R* to create a new word. Have other children read the other words on the chalkboard, changing them in the same way. Have the child read the new word.

Reading   Write the following sentences on sentence strips or on the chalkboard.

1. *Pete gave Pam the pie.*
2. *I picked a red rose.*
3. *My pet rat likes to run.*
4. *The ring is on the pen.*
5. *Pat petted the rabbit.*
6. *Peg will paint that room.*

In turn, invite volunteers to read each sentence and to name the words containing the *R* and the *P* sounds.

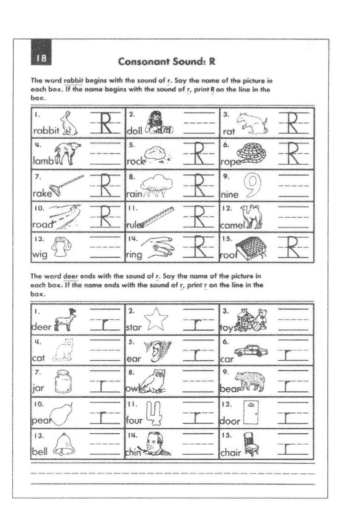

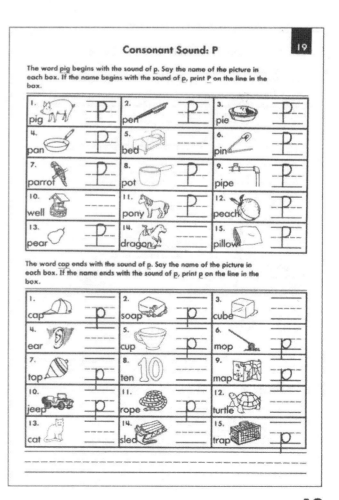

Reteaching

Forbidden-Letter Game   Invite the child to imagine a land where the consonant sound of *P* is forbidden. Challenge the child to name objects in the classroom that would be forbidden there (for example: pens, pencils). Extend the activity by changing the forbidden consonant sound to *R*.

Lesson 10
Consonant Sounds *V, QU, X, Y,* and *Z*   (pages 21–23)

Objective   The child will associate the letters *V, Qu, X, Y,* and *Z* with their consonant sounds.

Review

Listening   To provide practice identifying consonant sounds, write the following letters on the chalkboard: *S, T, B, H, J, M, K, F, G, D, L, N, W, C, R, P.* For each consonant sound, pronounce a word beginning with that sound. Suitable words include the following.

squirrel	*jam*	*gun*	*wagon*
tiger	*moon*	*door*	*camel*
basket	*key*	*lid*	*rabbit*
horse	*fan*	*nuts*	*pumpkin*

In turn, challenge the children to repeat each word after you and to circle the letter from the list that stands for the initial sound. Create a challenge by presenting the words in a random order.

Teaching Ideas

Listening/Speaking   Write the letters *V, Qu, X, Y,* and *Z* as column headings on the chalkboard. For each, invite a volunteer to name the consonant sound and to give one word that begins or that ends with that sound. As each appropriate suggestion is made, write the word on the chalkboard under the correct heading. You may wish to remind the children that in the English language the letter *Q* is always followed by the letter *u.* You might present the reminder in the form of a story.

> Q *is afraid to go anywhere without taking* u *along.*
> *So, everywhere we see the* Q, *we see* u *standing right beside it.*

You might also want to remind the children that while *Y* represents a consonant sound at the beginning of a word or syllable, *Y* represents another sound at the end of words. Explain to the children that they will learn about the other sound in future lessons.

Where's-the-*V*? Game   Invite three volunteers to participate in the first round of the game. Explain that the children will be listening for the position of the *V* sound in the following words: *glove, television, vacuum, lovely, varnish.* When a child correctly identifies the position of the *V* sound at the beginning, the middle, or the end of a word, assign one point. You might present an award ribbon for the *Super* V *Listener* to the child receiving the most points.

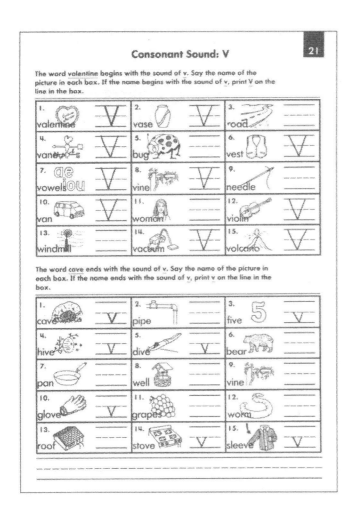

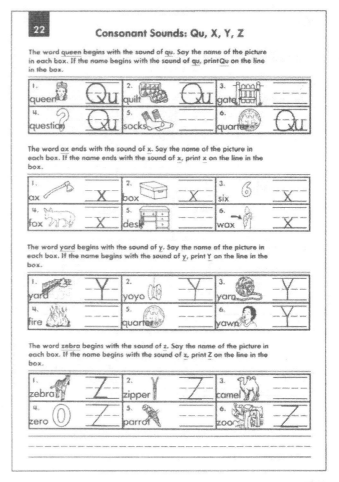

Continue additional rounds of the game using the following targeted sounds and words.

Qu: quiet, quarter, require, quart, request, quick

X: box, x-ray, sixteen, taxi, sixty, mix

Y: yet, yard, yeast, young, yams

Z: fuzz, wizard, zebra, breeze, zoo, lazy

Reading   Write the following sentences on the chalkboard or on sentence strips that can be placed in the pocket chart.

1. Did Uncle Vic drive the van into the yard?

2. The queen had a violet yo-yo.

3. Yes, it will be a quick visit to the zoo.

4. The fuzzy little duck made a quiet quack.

5. The dogs have to sleep in quite small boxes.

6. Zip up your coat and take your gloves.

For each, ask a child to read the sentence and to identify all of the words containing the consonant sounds *V, Qu, X, Y,* and *Z* by circling them.

Reteaching

Writing   Give the child sentence strips containing the above sentences. Have the child write *V, Qu, X, Y,* and *Z* as column headings on a sheet of paper. Challenge the child to write under each heading the words from the sentence that contain that sound. Praise the child, especially, for listing words with the targeted sound in the middle or at the end of a word.

Family Involvement Activity   Duplicate the Family Letter on page 101 of this Teacher's Edition. Send it home with the children.

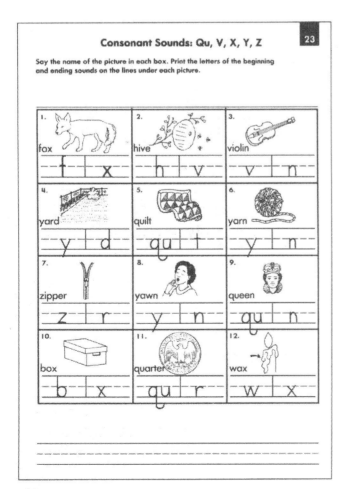

Lesson 11
Short Vowel A   (pages 24–27)

Objective   The child will apply the Short Vowel Rule to words containing the short vowel *A*.

Short Vowel Rule: If a word or syllable has only one vowel, and it comes at the beginning of the word or between two consonants, the vowel is usually short.

Review

Writing   To review ending consonant sounds, ask the children to write each ending consonant for the following words: *bag, cap, cat, hat, hand, fan*. Use pictures or sketch each object on the chalkboard. Above each picture, write the name of the object, omitting the final consonant but leaving a blank space or line for the letter. Invite volunteers to complete the words and to read each word aloud.

Teaching Ideas

Listening   Tell the children that the next group of lessons will review the short vowel sounds. Challenge the children to name the vowels. Then show a picture of a cat and pronounce the word *cat*. Ask a volunteer to repeat the short vowel sound heard in the word. Let the children know that the sound they hear in *cat* is the sound of the short *A*. You might refer to the pictures used in the Review. For each, ask a child to repeat after you the name of the object and to say the sound of *A* in the word.

Are-You-My-Partner? Game   Distribute the following word cards to the children: *bat, hat, sand, hand, ham, jam, mats, pats*. Have each child find a partner who has a card in which the word is the same except for the beginning letter. You might declare the first two children to find the correct partner as the winners. Invite them to be the first pair to read their words to the class and then to explain in their own words how both the words fit the Short Vowel Rule.

Reading   Write the following sentences on the chalkboard.

1. *Sam has a black pan.*
2. *Ann ran to Jack.*
3. *Hand Dad the ax, Pat.*
4. *Nan can run fast.*

For each, invite a volunteer to read a sentence and to circle all the short *A* words. Let children explain in their own words how each word fits the Short Vowel Rule.

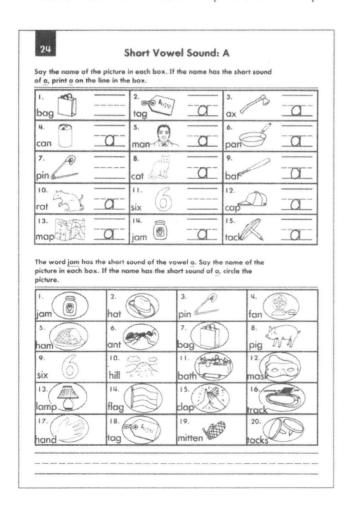

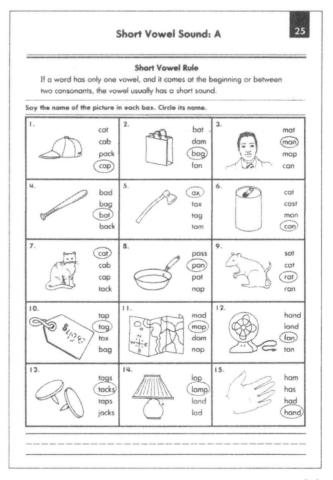

Extension

Research Have the child compile a list of the first names of the children in the class. (Lists saved from a similar activity in Lesson 8 may be reused.) Provide a few examples of names that contain the short *A* sound, such as *Sam, Ann, Pat*. Then challenge the child to examine the completed class list and to circle names that have the short *A* sound.

Reteaching

In-the-Bag Game Give the child a sheet of drawing paper and ask the child to draw a large bag. Explain that this bag will hold pictures of objects with names containing the short *A* sound. Then offer the child picture flashcards of the following items: *cap, cow, bed, pan, hat, ant, six, hand, foot, map*. Direct the child to write on the bag the name of each object with the short *A* sound. You might challenge the child to think up additional items that could go in the bag.

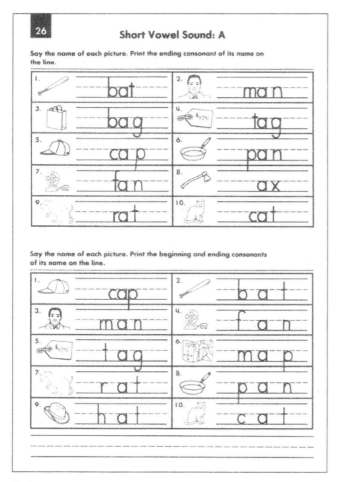

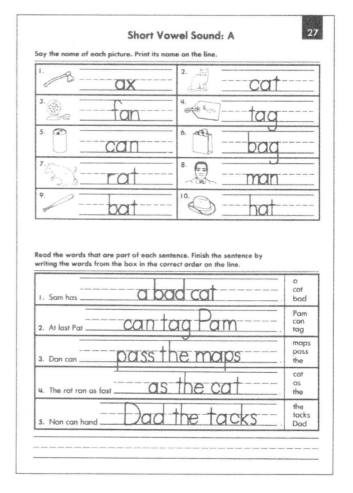

Lesson 12
Short Vowel *I* (pages 28–31)

Objective   The child will apply the Short Vowel Rule to words containing the short vowel *I*.

Review

Speaking   The following exercise may be used to review both the short *A* sound and some consonant sounds. Place word cards containing the following words on the chalkboard ledge: *bake, cat, ant, sail, back, pan, cake, ate, sand, pail*. Ask a volunteer to choose two words that have the same beginning letter. Then have the child tell which of the two words has the vowel sound of the short *A*. Continue in the same manner until all the pairs have been chosen. Encourage children to explain the Short Vowel Rule in their own words.

Teaching Ideas

Listening   To review the short *I* sound, write the following sentence on the chalkboard: *It is big*. Ask a volunteer to name the vowel that appears in each word and to tell what sound that vowel makes. Explain that the only vowel sound they hear in the sentence *It is big* is the sound of the short *I*.

Writing   Continue by pronouncing each of the following words: *in, his, pit, Jim, wig, hill*. For each word, invite a volunteer to write the word on the chalkboard and to tell why the *I* has the short vowel sound.

You might also want to challenge the children to think of names of people that contain the short *I* sound. Provide as an example the name *Jim*. Write down the suggested names, including the short *I* names of other children in the class.

Say-the-Word Game   Write the following incomplete words containing the short *I* sound on the chalkboard: *s __ ck, m __ lk, f __ st, r __ ng, g __ ft, l __ st, w __ ing*. Divide the children into two teams. Tell the children you will provide a question clue for each word on the chalkboard. You might give clues that have to do with meaning, such as: *Which word is the name of something good to drink?* Or, if you wish to reinforce consonant sounds, you could use phonics clues such as: *Which word begins with the consonant sound* F? Have the children raise their hands when they can identify the words. Award a point to the team that responds correctly first. Invite a child from that team to write the missing short *I* in the word on the chalkboard. Encourage the children to suggest words and clues that might be used in another round of the game.

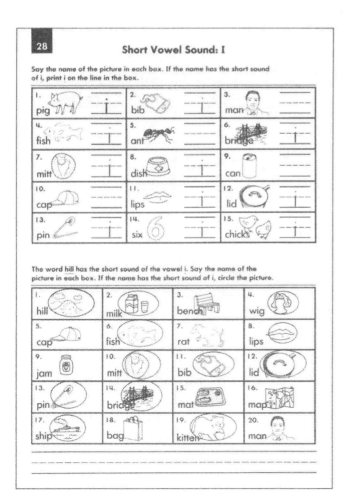

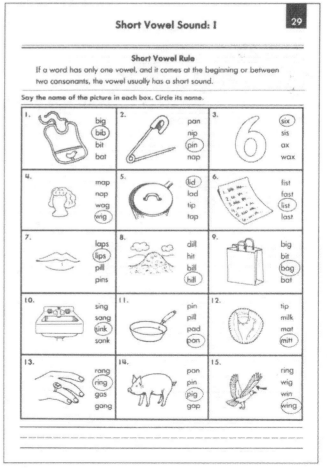

Reteaching

Reading   Write the following phrases on the chalk-board.

1. *will fill the bag*
2. *has six fans*
3. *will lick the pan*
4. *can fix it*
5. *is in the cab*

For each, ask the child to read the phrase and to draw a circle around the words that contain the short *A* sound. Then have the child draw a box around the short *I* words. (Save the phrases for use in the Extension activity that follows.)

Extension

Writing   Using the phrases from the Reteaching activity, challenge the child to think of names that contain the short *I* sound to place at the beginning of each phrase. Then have the child write out each complete sentence on a sheet of paper.

Sorting   The following critical thinking activity is useful for developing an awareness of the short *I* and the short *A* sounds. Write the following headings on the chalkboard: *Animals, Found in the Kitchen, Something to Wear.* Then distribute the following word cards: *ring, cat, pan, cap, rat, pig, lid, sink, milk, wig, hat, can, bib.* For each, have the child read the word and write it under the correct category.

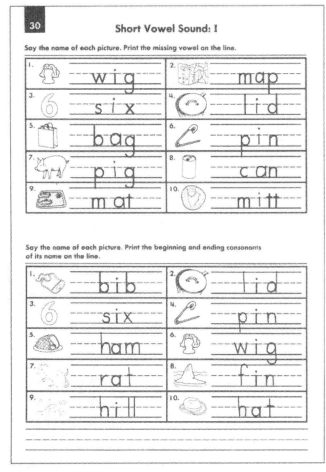

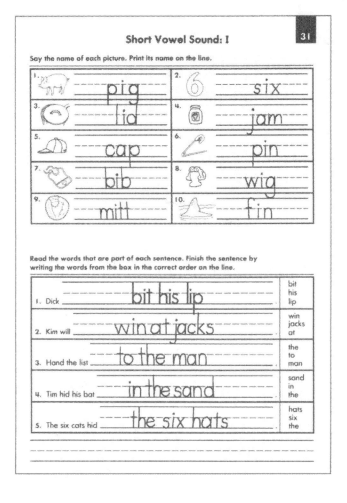

Lesson 13

Short Vowel *U*   (pages 32–35)

Objective   The child will apply the Short Vowel Rule to words containing the short vowel *U*.

Review

Say-the-Word Game   You might play the game described in Lesson 12 in this unit to practice recognition of the short vowel sounds of *A* and *I*. Write the following incomplete words on the chalkboard and provide meaning clues or phonics clues.

```
s__t     h__m     p__g     m__n
p__n     t_p      c__n     w__n
z__p     m__ss    f__x
```

You may wish to assign a bonus point to the team whose members correctly identify incomplete words in which both *A* and *I* can be used to make a word (*sit/sat, him/ham, pin/pan, tip/tap, zip/zap, miss/mass*).

Teaching Ideas

Listening   Introduce the short *U* sound by asking children in which direction you are pointing when you point to the ceiling. As they respond, write the word *up* on the chalkboard, and challenge a child to say just the *U* sound in the word *up*. Explain that this sound is the short *U* sound. You might

continue by saying the following words: *club, but, brush, plug, drum, nut*. In turn, invite volunteers to repeat each word after you and to identify the vowel sound. Challenge the children to explain how each word follows the Short Vowel Rule.

Reading   Write the following words on the chalkboard: *up, sun, us, bun, cup, bus*. Challenge three children to read two rhyming words from the list and to explain why the *U* has a short sound in each word. If a child has difficulty, invite another child to help out by explaining the Short Vowel Rule.

Print the following words and incomplete sentences on the chalkboard.

1. *I will sit in the* _____ .   *pup*
2. *Jack dug and* _____ .   *us*
3. *Pam does not see* _____ .   *up*
4. *Did you see Dan's* _____ ?   *sun*
5. *He can sit* _____ .   *dug*

For each, invite a volunteer to print the word that completes the sentence and to read the completed sentence aloud.

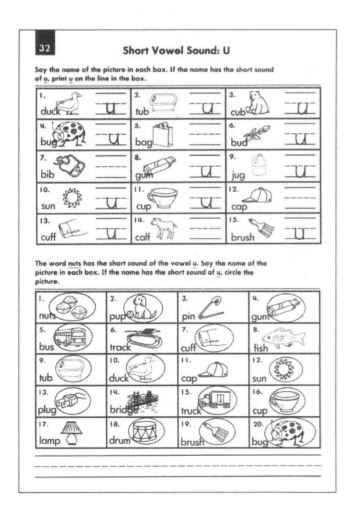

Extension

Reading   If a child needs more practice, you may wish to prepare sentence strips for the incomplete sentences in the previous activity. Then provide word cards containing the words that complete the sentences. Challenge the child to match each word card to the appropriate sentence. You may want to have the child copy the sentence.

Unscrambling Game   Create sets of three word cards for each of the following scrambled sentences: *gum/Tim/likes, run/can/pup, milk/likes/Sam, the/tub/fill, ham/the/cut, Kim/run/can*. Challenge the child to rearrange the cards in each set to create a short sentence. You might also ask the child to write and to read aloud the completed sentence.

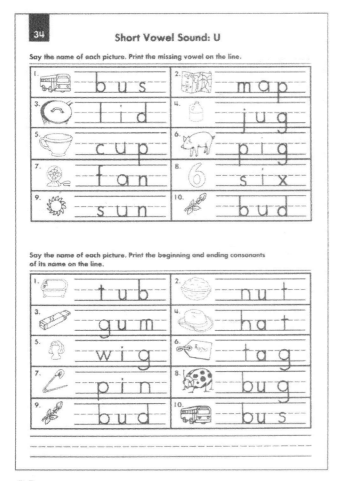

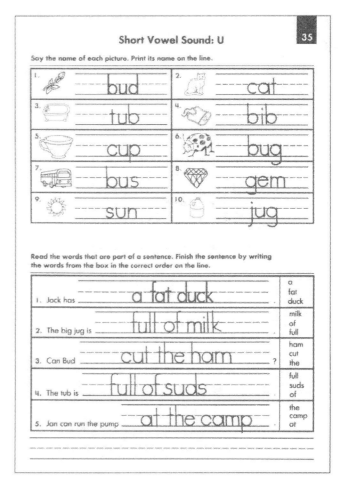

Lesson 14
Short Vowel O (pages 36–39)

Objective   The child will associate *O* with its short sound.

Review

Reading   Encourage recognition of short *A*, *I*, and *U* sounds by flashing the following word cards: *pal*, *mad*, *last*, *quick*, *wind*, *pill*, *bump*, *huff*, *pump*. For each card, call on a child to read the word and to identify the vowel.

Teaching Ideas

Listening   You might introduce the short *O* sound by turning the classroom lights off and on. Ask a child to describe what you have done. When a child gives the correct response, write the words *off* and *on* on the chalkboard. Invite a volunteer to give the sound of the vowel in the two words. Let the children know that the sound is the short *O* sound.

Sketch or show picture flashcards for the following objects: *box*, *dog*, *mop*, *top*. Ask a child to name each picture and to identify the vowel sound heard in each word.

Only-the-Short-*O* Game   Tell the children that Bob, Todd, and Bonnie belong to the Short *O* Club. Explain that each of these names contains the short *O* sound, and that the club members always use things that have the short *O* sound. Read aloud the following sets of choices.

a doll or a doughnut	*an ox or an ax*
a dot or a dart	*a pot or a pan*
a sock or a shoe	*a rock or a rack*
a cape or a clock	*a pot or a peanut*

For each, challenge a child to tell which of the two items members of the Short *O* Club would choose. If a child has difficulty deciding, you might write the two words on the chalkboard. To reinforce the lesson, ask children to explain why the selected word has the short *O* sound. Challenge the children to think of additional pairs of items for club members to choose. Be sure to point out that one choice should be a name that contains the short *O* sound while the other should be a name containing a different vowel sound.

Reading   Write the following sentences on the chalkboard or write them on sentence strips that you distribute to the children.

1. *Nan hid the doll in a box.*
2. *Tim will jump off the rock.*
3. *Bob had to pick up his socks.*
4. *Jin can fix the cut on her hand.*
5. *Don lost his cap in the mud.*

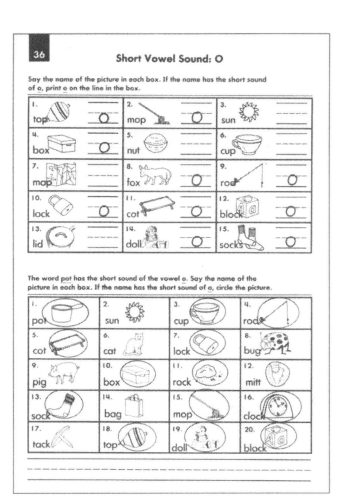

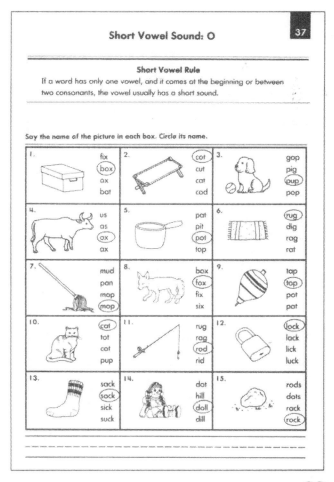

Invite volunteers to each read a sentence aloud and to name the short vowel words. To check comprehension and recognition of the short vowel sounds, you might ask questions similar to the following.

1. *Who had to pick up his socks?*
2. *What will Tim jump off?*
3. *What can Jin fix?*
4. *What did Nan hide?*
5. *What did Don lose?*
6. *Where did Don lose it?*

You might invite a child who has correctly identified all the short vowel sounds in a sentence to pose a question about the sentence for the other children.

Extension

Rhyming Game Prepare cards for the following words: *pot, cot, shop, mop, stop, top, box, fox, dog, log, bog, fog*. Shuffle the cards and then have the child sort the cards into pairs of rhyming words. Have the child read each pair to you, and invite the child to write a sentence using the rhyming word pair.

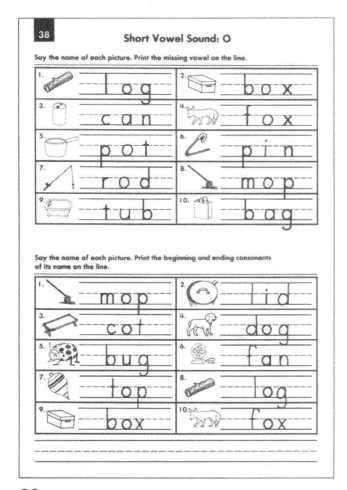

Lesson 15
Short Vowel *E* (pages 40–43)

Objective   The child will associate *E* with its short vowel sound.

Review

Riddle Game   To practice recognition of consonant and short vowel sounds, display picture flashcards for the following items: *ax, bag, hand, bib, lock, nuts, sun, clock, doll, mop*. Divide the children into teams. For each picture, provide a sound riddle, using the consonant sound rather than consonant letter name, such as the following: *Find the picture of a short I word that begins with the same sound as* big *does.* Assign a point for each correct response. You might offer a bonus point when a child is able to write the name of the picture.

Teaching Ideas

Listening   To introduce the short *E* sound, ask the children to tell what a spider spins. When a child gives the correct response, write the word *web* on the chalkboard. Let the children know that the vowel sound they hear in the word *web* is short *E*. Continue by providing picture flashcards for the following words: *bed, bell, belt, desk, hen, tent*. For each, call on a child to say the word and to give the vowel sound.

Speaking   To offer the children an opportunity to review the Short Vowel Rule for words with the short *E* sound, print the following words on the chalkboard: *jet, end, men, send, bet, desk*. Have a volunteer read the three words in the top row. Then challenge the child to identify the location of the vowel in each word and to explain why the *E* has the short sound. Have another child repeat the activity with the second row of words.

Reading   Print the following sentences on the chalkboard or on sentence strips.
   1. Get the pen for Fred.
   2. Ted held his little pet.
   3. Tell Bob to help Ed.
   4. Red Hen is in the nest.
   5. Peg can help Ted.
For each, invite a volunteer to read the sentence and to draw a ring around the short vowel *E* words in that sentence. Encourage children to say the Short Vowel Rule in their own words.

Say-the-Word Game   Play the Say-the-Word Game, as described in Lesson 12 in this unit, using words with the short *A, I, O, U*, and *E* sounds. Write the following incomplete words on the chalkboard: *p __ n, d __ sk, s __ n, m __ p, c __ t*. Because the children must make a choice between vowels, include clues for both a vowel sound and a meaning; for example: *If you add short O to this word, it will tell the name of something used to clean the floor* (mop).

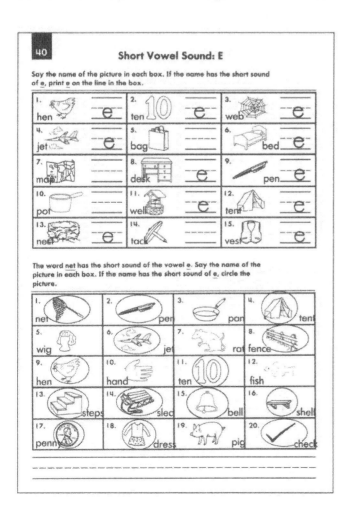

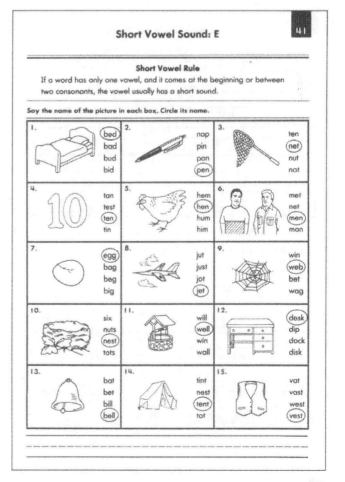

Extension

Research   To build greater awareness of words containing the short *E* vowel sound, challenge the child to write a list of names with the short *E* sound from the sentences in the prior reading activity. As a variation, invite the child to use a class list to identify names having the short *E* sound, as suggested in Lesson 8.

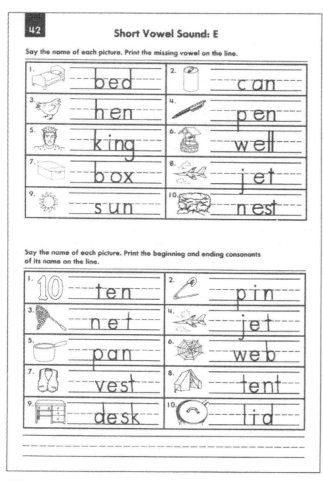

Lesson 16
Short Vowel Compound Words (pages 44–45)

Objective   The child will combine two short vowel words to form a compound word.

Review

Reading   To practice recognition of the short vowel words, print the following words on the chalkboard, inviting volunteers to each read a word and to identify its vowel sound: *sun, bag, hand, set, hill, tub, bath, top.*

Teaching Ideas

Listening   You might use the above words to introduce compound words. Draw a line from a word in the first column to a word in the second column to create appropriate compound words: *sunset, handbag, hilltop, bathtub.* To reinforce the children's understanding, print the new words on the chalkboard and have the children repeat each word. Explain that sometimes two words are combined to form a new, longer word and that such a word is called a compound word.

Speaking   You may wish to continue by printing the following compound words on the chalkboard: *bulldog, windmill, uphill, bobsled.* Invite a volunteer to draw a ring around each of the two small words in each compound word. Then challenge another volunteer to say the compound words and to use each word in a sentence.

Reading   Write the following words and incomplete sentences on the chalkboard.

1. *Tim lost his cat and got* _____ .   *sandbox*
2. *Sasha played in the* _____ .   *pigpen*
3. *At the farm we saw a* _____ .   *upset*

For each, invite a volunteer to find the compound word that completes the sentence. Then have the child print the word on the line and read the completed sentence.

Extension

Writing/Art   Present the child with a series of compound words such as the following: *sandbox, bulldog, sunset, bathtub, handbag.* Invite the child to write and illustrate an original sentence that uses at least one of the compound words.

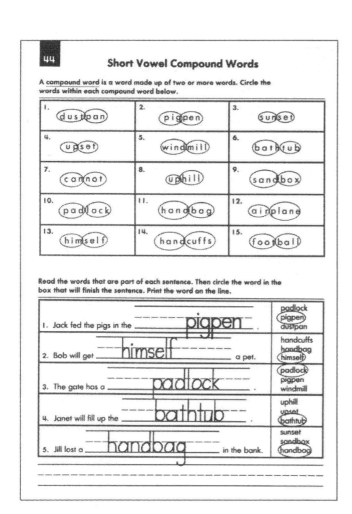

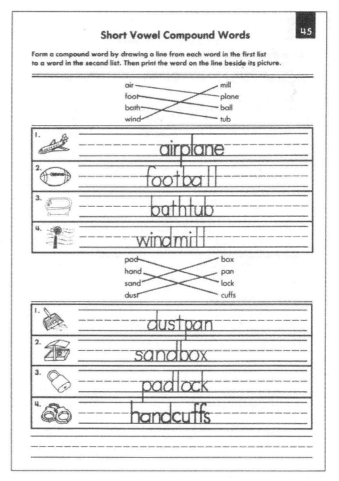

Lesson 17
Two-Syllable Words (page 46)

Objective   The child will identify each syllable in two-syllable words.

Review

Speaking   To practice recognition of compound words, write the following words on the chalkboard: *hand, self, him, bag, up, dog, bull, hill.* In turn, invite volunteers to form a compound word by drawing a line from a word in the first column to a word in the second column. Have the child say the compound word and use it in a sentence.

Teaching Ideas

Listening   To introduce the concept of two-syllable words that contain short syllables, print the following compound words on the chalkboard: *himself, handbag, uphill, bulldog.* Point out that these compound words from the Review are composed of two one-syllable words containing short vowels. Now have the children listen as you say each compound word slowly and ask them to tap once for each small word. Then write the following words on the chalkboard: *seven, wagon.* As you say each of these words, tap two times for the two parts. Explain that short words and small word parts like the *sev* and *en* in *seven* are called *syllables.* Draw a

diagonal line between the syllables in each of the words to show the two syllables.

Continue by writing the following words on the chalkboard: *basket, bonnet, mitten, until, muffin, tennis, rabbit, kitten.* For each, invite a volunteer to read the word, tap it, and tell the number of syllables. You might have all the children repeat the word and tap it to reinforce their awareness of syllabication. If a child has difficulty, demonstrate the tapping or invite another child to do so. Challenge a volunteer to divide the word into two syllables by drawing a diagonal line between the double consonant. Point out that each syllable in a word must have at least one vowel.

Reading   Write the following sentences on the chalkboard or on sentence strips.

1. *Ted has a bulldog.*
2. *He lifted me into the wagon.*
3. *Mom found the mitten.*
4. *We saw a kitten near the old windmill.*

For each, challenge a child to read the sentence and to write above each word the number of syllables it has. Encourage children who give incorrect responses by tapping problematic words for them.

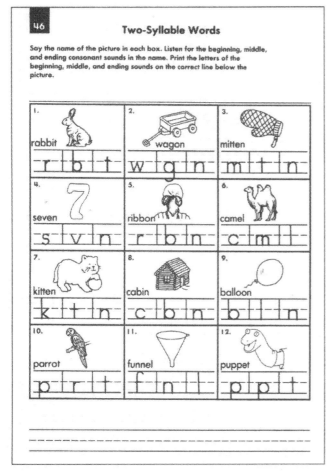

Unit 4 Long Vowels

Lesson 18
Long Vowel A (pages 47–50)

Objective The child will identify the long sound of *A* in isolation and within words.

Long Vowel Rule 1: If one syllable has two vowels, the first vowel is usually long and the second is usually silent.

Review

Listening To practice recognition of both compound words and syllables, ask the children to listen for the syllables in the following words: *baseball, sailboat, lakeside, rainbow, gatepost*. As you pronounce each word, invite a volunteer to tell how many syllables are in the word. (If a child has difficulty, encourage the child to tap out the syllables while saying the word.) Then write the word on the chalkboard and invite another child to mark the break between the two syllables with a diagonal line.

Teaching Ideas

Speaking/Listening Point out that the first syllable in each of the compound words in the Review exercise contains the same vowel sound. Then explain to the children that this vowel sound is the same one they heard at the beginning of the word *cake*. Identify the sound as long vowel *A* and invite a volunteer to pronounce just the sound.

You might take this opportunity to review Long Vowel Rule 1. For each of the compound words in the Review exercise, invite a child to erase the second syllable and to read the one-syllable word left on the chalkboard. Have another child underline all the vowels in the remaining word and identify their sounds.

Are-You-My-Partner? Game Distribute word cards containing the following words: *tap, tape, can, cane, at, ate, cap, cape*. Explain that the children are to locate a partner whose word card has a word that is spelled with the same consonants but has a different vowel sound. Appoint the first two children to pair up correctly as the winners. Invite all the partners to show their word cards to the class, read their two words, and then explain why one of their word cards has the long vowel sound. Invite volunteers to each use one of the long vowel words in a sentence. Challenge children to think of a sentence that uses both the short vowel and the long vowel word.

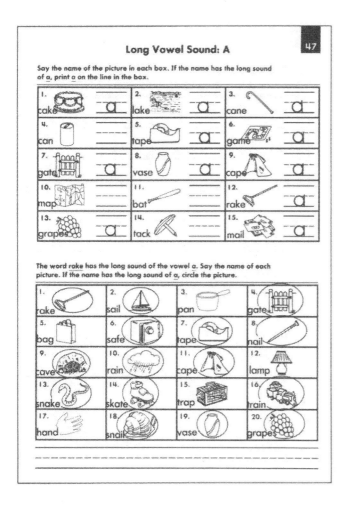

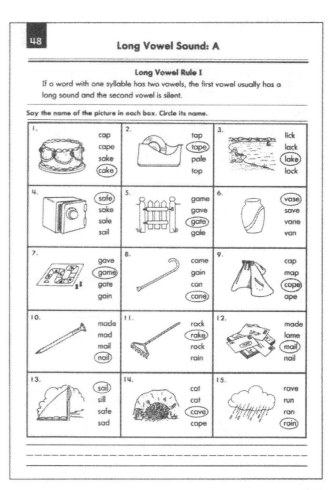

Extension

Writing Write the following words as column headings on the chalkboard: *cake, game, mail.* Below each word, have the child write two or three rhyming words. Then encourage the child to write sentences using each set of rhyming long *A* words. Let the child know that "silly sentences" are permissible. You might also invite the child to illustrate the sentences.

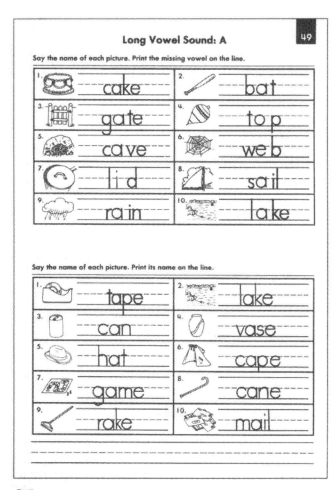

Lesson 19
Long Vowel I (pages 51–54)

Objective   The child will identify the long sound of *I* in isolation and within words.

Review

Listening   To develop auditory discrimination of the long *A* and short vowel sounds, pronounce the following words and ask a volunteer to identify the vowel sound in each: *fox, cat, cane, made, ate, lid, damp, cape, late, wake, it.*

Teaching Ideas

Speaking   You might begin by asking what frozen water is called. When a child gives the correct response, write the word *ice* on the chalkboard. Ask the child to identify the vowel sound heard at the beginning of the word. Continue by sketching or showing picture flashcards for each of the following objects: *bike, fire, kite, pie, pipe.* For each, invite a child to repeat the word and to tell the vowel sound.

Writing   Write the following words on the chalkboard: *pin, hid, win, bit, rip, dim.* For each, invite a volunteer to read the word and to add an *E* to the end of the word. Then have another child read the new word. Praise children who offer Long Vowel Rule 1 as an explanation for the long vowel sound in the new words.

Reading   Write the following sentences on the chalkboard.

1. *Tim likes to dive in the lake.*
2. *I will ride on the bike.*
3. *Can I paint the slide?*
4. *It is a nine-mile hike to the camp.*
5. *Kim will tie up a pile of vines.*

For each, invite a volunteer to read the sentence aloud and to circle words that contain long vowel sounds.

Extension

Only-the-Long-I Game   Tell the child that Brian, Mike, and Dinah all belong to the Long *I* Club. Explain that each of these names contains the long *I* sound, and that the club members always use things with names that have the long

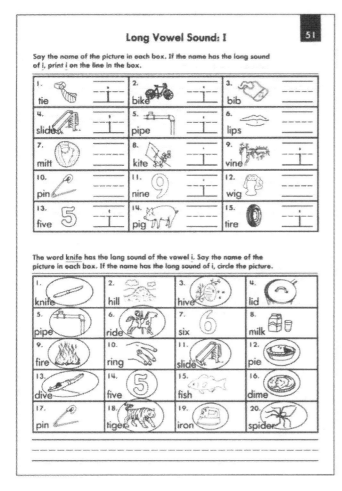

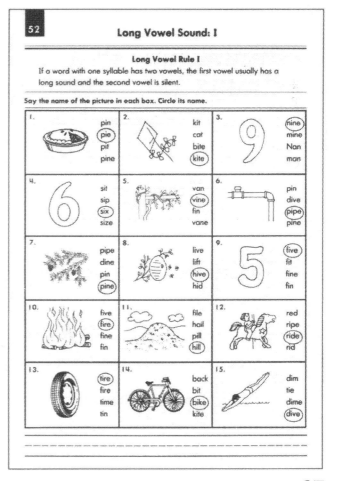

I sound. Have the child decide which item from each of the following pairs club members would choose: *a bike or skates, a quarter or a dime, a pie or a cake, a pin or a tie.* You might challenge the child to provide additional choices for club members. Remind the child that in each pair, one name should have the long sound of *I,* and the other name should have a different vowel sound. Write each suggested pair on the chalkboard so that the child can see how each long *I* word is spelled.

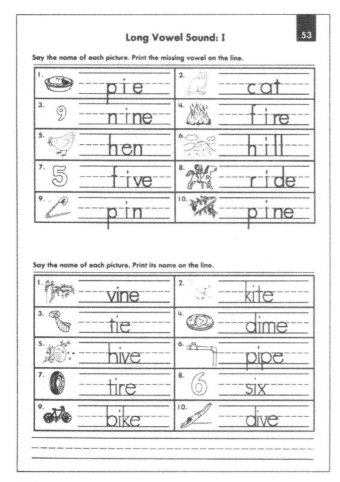

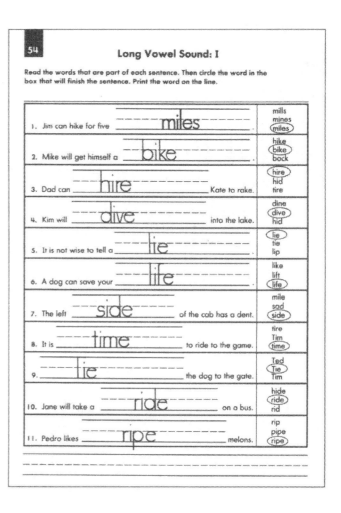

Lesson 20

Long Vowel *U*   (pages 55–57)

Objective   The child will identify the long sound of *U* in isolation and within words.

Review

Reading   To practice recognition of long and short vowel words, prepare a letter card for small *e*. As you show the card to the children, tell them that *e* can give "Word-Changer" powers. Write the following words on the chalkboard: *pin, at, kit, slid, Tim, cap, rid, mad*. For each, invite a volunteer to read the word. Then invite the child to become a "Word-Changer" by holding the letter card next to the word on the chalkboard. Encourage the child to read the new long vowel word.

Teaching Ideas

Reading   You may wish to build on the Review exercise by writing *us* on the chalkboard. Ask a child to read the word and to use the "Word-Changer" card to form the word *use*. Identify the vowel sound at the beginning of the word as the long sound of *U*. Continue by writing the following words on the chalkboard: *cut, cub, tub*. For each, invite a child to act as a "Word-Changer." Challenge the children to explain why the vowel sound changes in each word. Encourage children to explain Long Vowel Rule 1 in their own words.

For additional practice, present the following word cards: *fuse, June, Sue, suit, mule, tune*. For each, invite a volunteer to read the word, identify the vowels, and then name the vowel sound heard. Encourage the children to express Long Vowel Rule 1 in their own words.

Sensible-Sentence Game   For further practice using long *U* words, prepare and distribute strips for the following incomplete sentences.

1. *June can hum a funny _____ .*
2. *Luke will ride the gray _____ .*
3. *Put another ice _____ in that cup.*
4. *Sue has a cute blue _____ .*

In addition, prepare and distribute word cards containing the following words: *mule, tune, suit, cube*.

Explain to the children that each of them is to seek out and stand with another child whose word or incomplete sentence combines with their own to form a sensible sentence. After all the pairs have formed, ask one partner in each pair to read the completed sentence and the other partner to identify the long *U* words. (Save the sentence strips for use in the Reteaching activity that follows.)

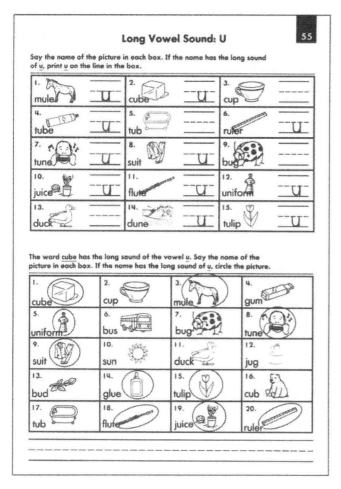

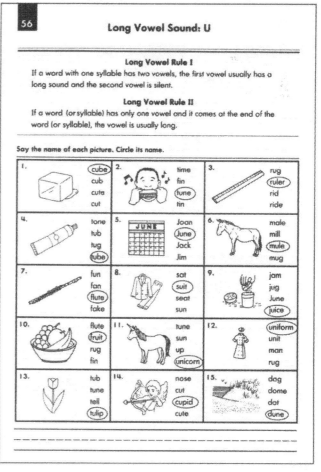

Reteaching

Reading   Challenge the child to form "silly sentences" using the sentence strips and word cards from the previous exercise. Have the child read each sentence aloud. Encourage the child to identify the words with the long *U* sound and to apply Long Vowel Rule 1 to these words. You might also have the child illustrate one of the "silly sentences."

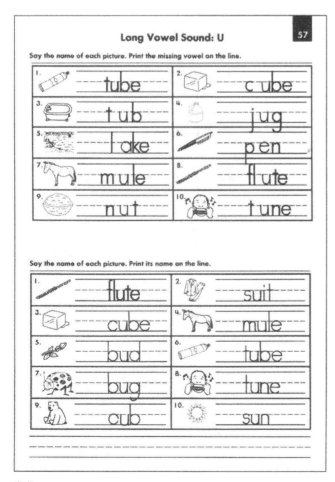

Lesson 21
Long Vowel *O* (pages 58–61)

Objective   The child will identify the long sound of *O* in isolation and within words.

Review

Writing   To practice recognition of long and short vowel words, sketch pictures or display picture flashcards of the following objects: *cap, hat, tub*. For each, invite a volunteer to print the name of the picture on the chalkboard. Then have another child add a silent *E* to the end of the word and read the new long vowel word.

Teaching Ideas

Listening   Ask the children to name a word opposite in meaning to the word *shut*. When a child gives the correct response, write the word *open* on the chalkboard and identify the beginning sound as the sound of long vowel *O*. Continue by reading the following list, asking the children to raise their hands each time they hear a name that contains the sound of long *O*: *Joe, Tom, Toni, Bob, Jon, Oprah, Joan, Lois, Monty*.

Pick-Your-Sides Game   Distribute word cards for the following words: *mop, box, top, doll, boat, coat, goat, hoe, nose, cone*. For each word card, have a child identify the word and the vowel sound. If the word on the word card includes the short *O* sound, have the child stand on the left side of the classroom; if the word has the long *O* sound, have the child stand on the right side of the classroom. After these children have chosen the appropriate place to stand, collect their word cards and then redistribute them to other children. Repeat the procedure.

Speaking   Write the following words on the chalkboard: *toad, hot, hose, coal, hop, hope, pot, pole*. For each, challenge a volunteer to read the word, tell if the vowel sound is long or short, and explain why. If a child needs guidance, have the child circle the vowel that can be heard in each word.

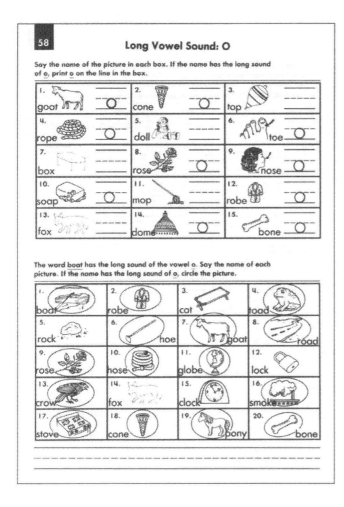

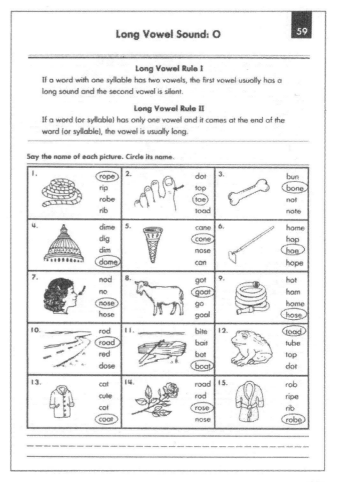

41

Extension

Long-*O*-Then-Go Game   Prepare word cards for the following: *cube, foam, rail, life, hoe, dot, note, nod, got, goat, hot, boat, toad, bite, tube, road*. As you hold up each word card, direct the child to read each word silently. Explain that if the word has the long *O* sound, the child may take a step forward; but if the word does not have the long *O* sound, the child must freeze. Point out that an incorrect move will send the child back to the starting line. Let the game conclude when the child successfully travels to a designated finish line.

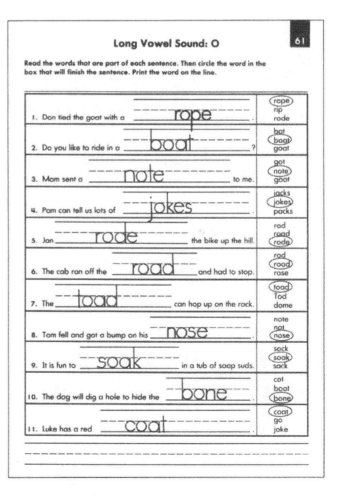

Lesson 22
Long Vowel *E*   (pages 62–65)

Objective   The child will apply Long Vowel Rule 1 to identify the long *E* sound in isolation and within words.

Review

Spelling Game   To review short and long vowels *A*, *I*, *U*, and *O*, write the following words on the chalkboard: *jump, use, rain, kite, box, nose, kit, ran.* Invite a volunteer to point to one of the words, spell it, and then read the word. Allow this child to choose a second child to identify the vowel sound in each word. Encourage the second child to choose a third child to give the rule governing that vowel sound. (You may wish to write the vowel rules on the chalkboard and number them to allow the children to refer to the rules by number.) Continue play until all the words have been identified. To include as many children as possible, encourage each volunteer to choose classmates who have not yet had a turn. Extend the game by listing additional words.

Teaching Ideas

Listening   Place picture flashcards of the following words on the chalkboard ledge or in a pocket chart: *eagle, beads, bee, jeep, leaf.* (These picture flashcards may be prepared prior to the lesson, or if you prefer, simple drawings

on the chalkboard may be used.) For each, have a child say the name of the picture and then identify the vowel sound heard in each name. Emphasize that the sound heard in each word is the sound of long *E*.

Writing   Write the following pairs of words on the chalkboard: *met/meat, bed/bead, Ben/bean, set/seat, red/read, fed/feed.* Encourage the children to listen for the short and long sounds of *E* as you read each pair of words. Challenge the children to explain why the *E* has a short sound in one word and a long sound in the other. (You might first review the vowel rules by using the questions outlined in Lessons 11 and 18 of this unit.) For each word pair, ask a child to draw a circle around the letter that makes the short *E* sound and a line under the two letters that make the long *E* sound. (You may wish to use different colors of chalk to add interest or to encourage those students who are reluctant to participate.) To continue the lesson, write the following incomplete sentences and words on the chalkboard.

1. *Eve had to go to* _____ .	*bed*	*bead*
2. *Jean sat in the back* _____ .	*set*	*seat*
3. *Did Lee cook the* _____ ?	*met*	*meat*
4. *Sue's dog is not* _____ .	*fed*	*feed*
5. *Tell Ben to eat the* _____ .	*bets*	*beets*

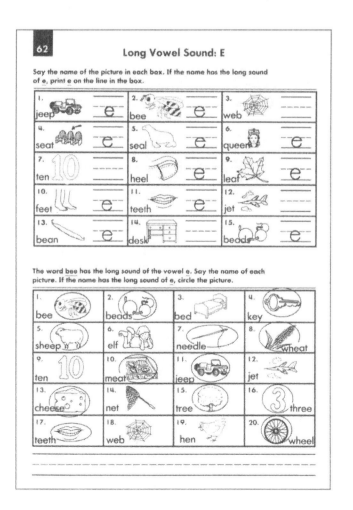

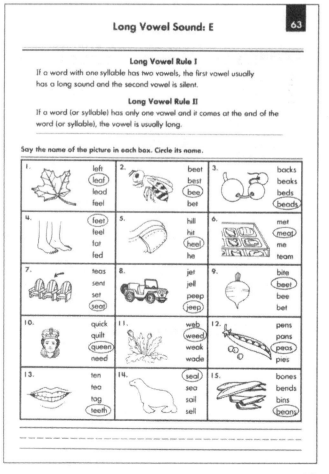

43

Invite volunteers to come to the chalkboard and to circle the word to the right of each sentence that completes the sentence. Encourage the children to read the completed sentences, listening for the sound of *E*. (You may also want to have the children tell whether the completion word is a long or short vowel word.)

Extension

Ball Game Invite the child to play the Ball Game. Draw several circles to represent balls on the chalkboard, and write a word containing a short or a long vowel sound in each "ball." Explain that the child may "catch" a ball by reading the word on it, naming the vowel, and telling whether the vowel has a short or long sound. Challenge the child to create an additional ball for each one that is caught by drawing a circle and writing a word that contains the same vowel sound.

Family Involvement Activity Duplicate the Family Letter on page 103 of this Teacher's Edition. Send it home with the children.

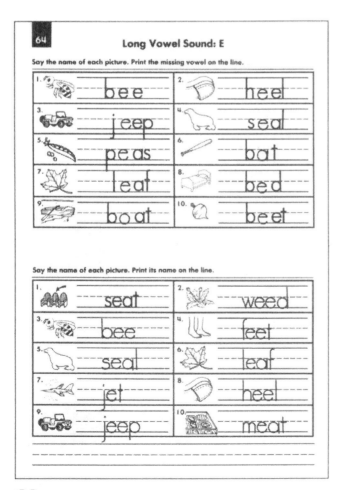

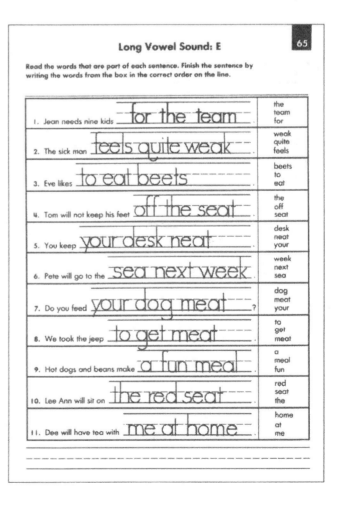

Lesson 23
Two-Syllable Words   (pages 66–68)

Objective   The child will read two-syllable words and identify each syllable containing long and short vowels.

Review

Writing   Write the following incomplete words on the chalkboard.

```
r__de    s__d    f__ne    l__ck
b__t     l__ke   r__pe    qu__ck
f__ll    r__p    w__de    n__t
```

Ask a volunteer to complete each word by writing an appropriate vowel in the blank. Challenge the rest of the children to read each completed word.

Teaching Ideas

Writing   Write the following columns of syllables on the chalkboard.

```
rab    fin
nap    pet
muf    kin
pup    bit
```

Explain to the children that a syllable is a part of a word and each syllable contains one vowel sound. (You may then wish to reinforce this concept by providing the word *rabbit* as an example on the chalkboard and dividing it into syllables.) In turn, ask volunteers to draw a line from a syllable in the first column to the syllable in the second column that completes the word. Challenge each child to read the new word.

Continue the lesson by writing the following compound words on the chalkboard: *uphill, raincoat, homemade, cannot, teapot, pipeline, suntan, lifeboat, oatmeal*. Explain to the children that these compound words are made up of two smaller words, and that each of these words is a syllable. For each compound word, ask a child to draw a ring around each syllable.

Complete-the-Compound Game   Write compound words on strips of tagboard or construction paper. Cut the strips in half at the point where the compound word could be divided into syllables. Distribute the syllable strips randomly to the children. Explain to the children that they are to seek out and stand with the person who has the syllable strip to complete each compound word. (If children have difficulty finding their partners, you may reference the compound words that were used on the chalkboard.) Draw aside partners to make the selection easier for those who remain unmatched.

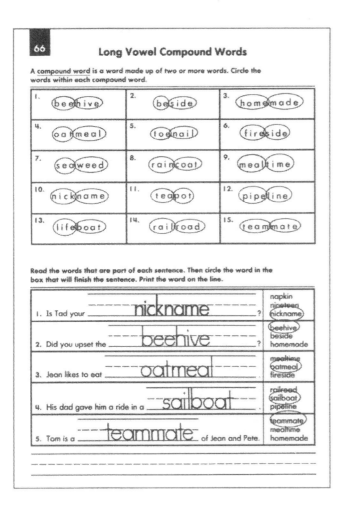

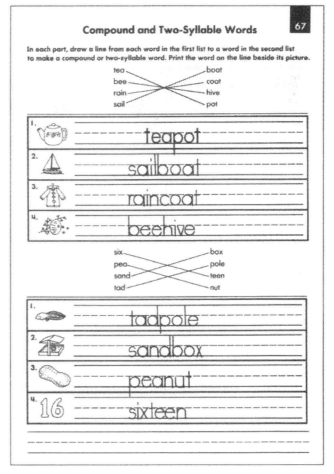

45

Extension

Writing   Write the following sentences on the chalk-board.

  1. He left his raincoat on the airplane.
  2. The oatmeal cookies are homemade.
  3. There are peanuts in the cupcakes.

Invite the child to read the first sentence. Encourage the child to circle and to name the two words that make up each compound word. Finally, challenge the child to name the vowel sound in each syllable of the compound words. Continue with the remaining sentences. You may then wish to ask the child to write more sentences using compound words. The child could write the sentences on the chalkboard or on a sheet of paper. You might then repeat the exercise, using the sentences the child has created.

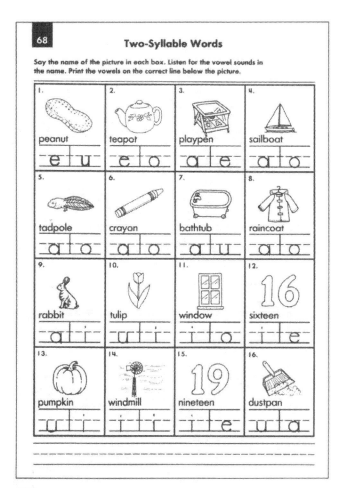

Lesson 24

R Blends (pages 69–71)

Objective The child will identify the sounds of *r* blends.

A consonant blend is two or three consonants sounded together in which the sound of each letter can be heard.

Review

Speaking To practice recognition of long and short vowel sounds, write the following words on the chalkboard: *tip, tape, tack, maid, meat, mess, mint, need, ride, hog, tank, toss.* (Save the words for use later in the lesson.) Invite the children to read each word aloud. Ask the children to identify the vowel sound they hear in each word. For each word, challenge the children to apply the Long or the Short Vowel Rule. (You may want to reference the rules on the chalkboard to assist the children.)

Teaching Ideas

Listening Write the following words on the chalkboard: *trick, drive, press, frame, crack, grip, break.* Invite the children to listen for the beginning sound in each of the words as you say them aloud. Explain to the children that each of the words begins with an *r* blend. (Stress that an *r* blend consists of a consonant and *r* and that both consonant sounds can be heard.) Encourage the children to repeat the words after you and to identify the *r* blend in each word.

Writing Invite the children to make a list of *r* blends (for example: *tr, br, gr, dr, fr, cr*). Record the list of blends on the chalkboard. Then, using the list of words from the Review, have the children form new words by replacing the initial consonant with an *r* blend. For example, *tip* would become *trip.* (You may wish to have children come to the chalkboard to change the words, or each child could record the new words on a sheet of paper.) Finally, encourage the children to underline the *r* blends in each word.

Art You might have the children find pictures in magazines of objects with names that begin with an *r* blend. Possibilities include the following: *train, fruit, grapes, dress, crib, tree, bridge, drum.* Encourage the children to make picture flashcards by cutting out and pasting their *r* blend pictures on small squares of tagboard or construction paper. Have each child print the name of the picture at the bottom of the square, underlining the *r* blend. (Assist children who have difficulty spelling their picture words.) Encourage the chil-

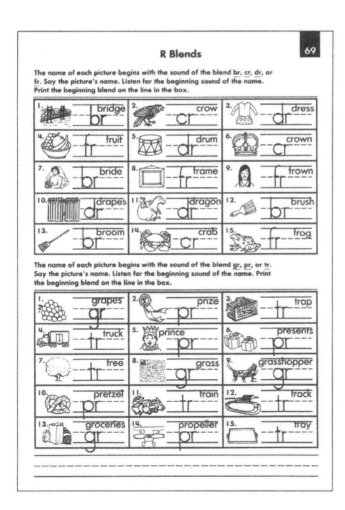

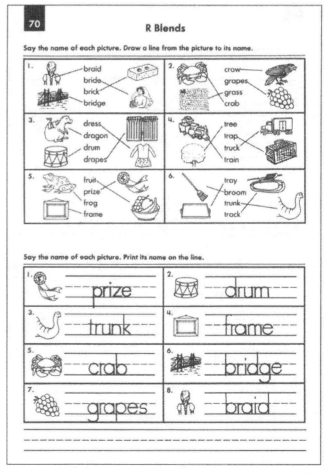

dren to share their picture flashcards with the rest of the class and to name the picture and its *r* blend. (These cards may be saved for future use.)

Extension

Tactile   Cut the letter shapes of *r* blends *tr, br, gr, dr, fr, cr,* and *pr* out of corrugated cardboard or sandpaper. Encourage the child to trace the blends with a finger and to say each blend's name while tracing. Have the child trace the blend on a sheet of construction paper with a crayon or marker. Then challenge the child to name a word in which the blend is heard and to record the word on the construction paper. Invite the child to repeat the process using another blend.

Writing   Write the following words on the chalkboard: *prize, drum, truck, trunk, crab, prince.* Say each word, encouraging the child to repeat the words after you. Invite the child to trace over the *r* blends at the beginning of each word.

R Blends   71

Read the words that are part of each sentence. Then circle the word in the box that will finish the sentence. Print the word on the line.

1. Eve likes to win __prizes__ .	press, (prizes), grass
2. The dog will __drink__ from the creek.	dream, (drink), track
3. Sue __freed__ the cub from the trap.	fried, (freed), trade
4. I will __trade__ bikes with you.	(trade), drain, trap
5. Give me the tube of hand __cream__ near the sink.	crib, (cream), dream
6. My train fell off the track and __broke__ .	(broke), croak, braid
7. __Print__ your name inside your coat.	Prize, Trip, (Print)
8. Use care if you __cross__ the road.	press, (cross), grass
9. Dad will bring gifts back from his __trip__ .	trap, (trip), drip
10. The ants made a trail to the __crack__ in the tree.	trick, track, (crack)
11. The __frog__ jumped away.	brick, (frog), from

48

Lesson 25
L Blends (pages 72–74)

Objective   The child will identify the sounds of *l* blends.

Review

Writing   To practice recognition of two-syllable words, print the following words on the chalkboard.

cracking	*treehouse*	*bridesmaid*
braided	*crossing*	*printed*
dragon	*nosedrops*	*driveway*

Have a volunteer point to one of the words, read it, and draw a ring around each of its two syllables. (You may wish to remind the children that each syllable must have at least one vowel sound.) Then ask the child to underline the vowel in each syllable. Challenge all the children to say the word again, clapping their hands for each syllable. Follow the same procedure for each of the other words.

Teaching Ideas

Listening   Write the following words on the chalkboard: *flat, blow, fly, plane, glow, glad, clay, please, blanket.* Invite the children to listen for the beginning sound in each of the words as you say them aloud. Ask the children to identify the sound they hear at the beginning of each word. Explain that the sound heard is the sound of an *l* blend. (You may wish to stress that an *l* blend consists of a consonant and an *l* and that both consonant sounds can be heard.) Encourage the children to repeat the words after you, listening for the *l* blend in each word.

Writing   Place the following picture flashcards on the chalkboard ledge: *block, clock, flowers, glass, plant.* (These picture flashcards may be prepared by you prior to the lesson, or the cards can be made by the children as part of the lesson. Simple sketches on the chalkboard might also be used.) Invite a volunteer to identify each picture and print its name on the chalkboard. Have another child read each word again, identify the letters used in the *l* blend, and use the word in a sentence. You may wish to record the sentences on the chalkboard or strips of paper.

To continue, print the following sentences on the chalkboard.

1. *Glen has a blue and green flag.*
2. *Fred, please clean the playpen.*
3. *The flock of ducks ate the grain.*
4. *Clem drank his glass of water.*
5. *Here is the glass near the flat plate.*

In turn, ask volunteers to each read a sentence aloud, drawing a box around each word that has an *l* blend, and a ring around each word that has an *r* blend. (Encourage children who are reluctant to participate by using different colors of chalk and allowing the children to choose the color they prefer.)

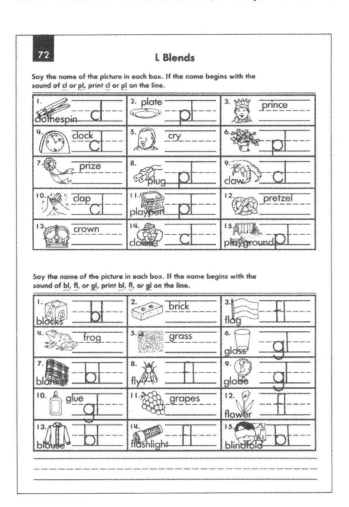

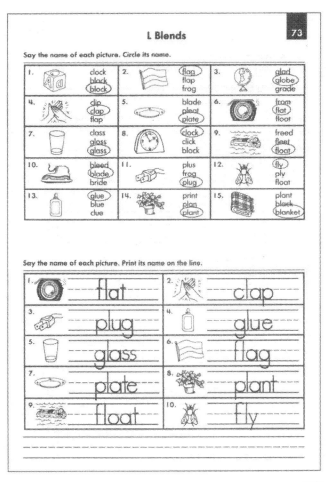

Reteaching

Speaking   Write the following words on the chalkboard: *blend, clock, flowers, glass, plant.* Say the words aloud, emphasizing the *l* blend. Invite the child to watch the movement of your mouth and lips as you say the words. Encourage the child to repeat the words as you say them again. You may want to have the child try this exercise in front of a mirror so the movement of the mouth and lips can be observed. (Save the words for use in the writing activity that follows.)

Writing   Using the previous words, encourage the child to identify the two consonants that make up the *l* blend. Allow the child to trace over the *l* blend with chalk or with a finger. Finally, invite the child to read the words again, listening for the *l* blend in each word.

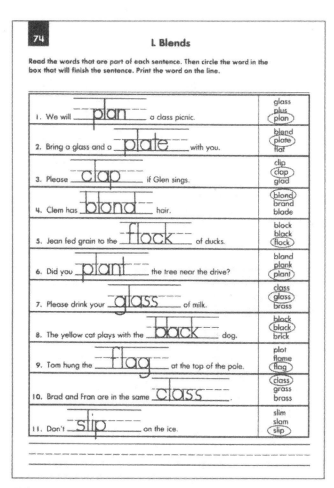

Lesson 26
S Blends (pages 75–77)

Objective   The child will identify the sounds of *s* blends.

Review

Which-Blend-Do-You-Hear? Game   Review the *r* and *l* blends by printing the following blends on small squares of tagboard or construction paper: *bl, gl, dr, fl, fr, pl, br, gr, cl, tr, pr, cr.* (The cards may be prepared by you ahead of time or by the children as part of the lesson.) Begin the game by placing the blend cards along the chalkboard ledge. Invite the children to identify the blend in the word *dried*. Ask a volunteer to hold up the card for *dr* and to name the consonants in the blend. Continue the game with the following words: *trap, plan, print, dream, clap, float, cream, blade, glue, frame, clock, grass, broom.* You may wish to extend the game by challenging the children to think of additional words for each blend.

Teaching Ideas

Listening   Write the following words on the chalkboard: *skates, smoke, snail, spring, spoon, stamp, strawberries, swing, sled.* Invite the children to listen for the beginning sound in each word as you read it aloud. Tell the children the sound they hear at the beginning of each word is an *s* blend.

(Stress that an *s* blend consists of one or more consonants and an *s*, and that the sound of each letter can be heard.) Invite volunteers to each read one of the words aloud. Challenge them to name the *s* blend heard in each.

Writing   Have each child copy the list of words on a sheet of paper. Encourage the children to use red crayons or markers to trace the *s* blends in each word. (You may wish to ask one child to trace the *s* blends in the words on the chalkboard to provide a reference for those children at their seats.)

Write the following incomplete sentences and word clues on the chalkboard.

1. *Tom can _____ his top fast.*   *street*
2. *Glen rode his bike up the _____.*   *Spring*
3. *Eat a _____ before bed.*   *spin*
4. *_____ rains fill the puddles.*   *swept*
5. *Bill _____ the driveway.*   *snack*

For each sentence, have a volunteer select the word from the list that completes the sentence. Have each child read the completed sentence and circle the *s* blend in the word.

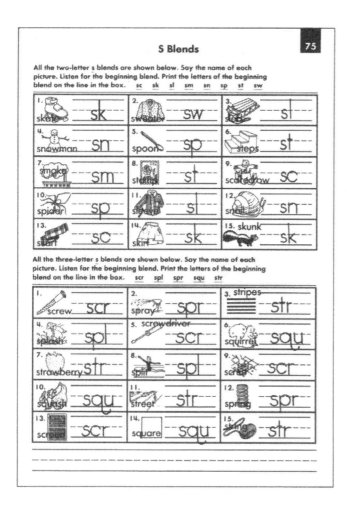

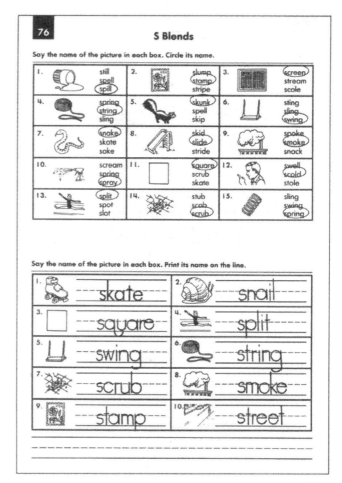

Extension

Writing Write the word *rib* on the chalkboard. Invite the child to say the word aloud. Explain to the child that you are going to make a new word from the word *rib* by adding a letter to the beginning of the word. Add the letter *c* to the beginning of *rib* to make the word *crib*. Encourage the child to read the new word. Stress that the word *crib* begins with a consonant blend. Invite the child to trace the consonant blend. Continue the activity with the following words.

wing/swing	*rain/train*	*lean/clean*
late/plate	*rake/brake*	*mile/smile*
team/steam	*row/crow*	*lad/glad*

S Blends

Read the words that are part of each sentence. Finish the sentence by writing the words from the box in the correct order on the line.

1. The cat likes to	scare the dog	the dog scare
2. Dad can	swim a mile	mile a swim
3. Do you like to	smell the tulips ?	the smell tulips
4. Stan likes to go	to the stream	the stream to
5. The frog in the pond	made a splash	splash made a
6. Clean the spot	off your sleeve	your sleeve off
7. I help my father	scrub the floor	the floor scrub
8. Can you spin the top	in the square ?	square in the
9. I can do tricks	on my skates	my on skates
10. Jim fell and	sprained his toe	toe sprained his
11. Green means go and	red means stop	means red stop

52

Lesson 27
Y as a Vowel   (pages 78–79)

Objective   The child will apply Vowel *Y* Rules to identify the sound of *Y* in words.

Vowel *Y* Rules: When *Y* is the only vowel at the end of a one-syllable word, it has the long sound of *I*.

When *Y* is the only vowel at the end of a word of more than one syllable, it has the sound of long *E*.

Review

To review the sound of consonant *Y*, write the following sentences on the chalkboard.

1. *Would you like to see Tom's yo-yo?*
2. *Yes, you can go to camp next year.*
3. *It is not yet time to beat the yellow drum.*

Have volunteers circle the words that begin with *Y* in each sentence.

Teaching Ideas

Speaking   Write the letters *A, E, I, O,* and *U* on the chalkboard. Have the children identify the letters as vowels. Write the letter *Y* next to the vowels. Explain to the children that when *Y* appears at the end of a word, it is considered a vowel. Point out that vowel *Y* can represent the sound of long *I* or the sound of long *E*. Continue by printing the following words on the chalkboard: *cry, dry, fry, bunny, dolly, pony.* For each word, ask a volunteer to read the word aloud, tell the number of syllables, and identify the sound of *Y*. Explain the Vowel *Y* Rules. Refer the children to the words on the chalkboard. For each word, encourage the children to apply the Vowel *Y* Rules to explain the sound of *Y*.

Writing   Write the following words on the chalkboard: *fly, candy, silly, spy, by, puppy, lady, my.* For each word, ask a volunteer to come to the chalkboard, read the word, and write the vowel sound *Y* represents, using *E* for long *E* sound and *I* for long *I* sound.

Then write the following sentences on the chalkboard.

1. *My baby likes to play pattycake.*
2. *Sally will try to ride the pony.*
3. *Jimmy spoke softly to the shy puppy.*
4. *The yellow cat sat by my tiny stuffed bunny.*

Invite a volunteer to come to the chalkboard and to read the first sentence. Have the child invite a classmate to underline the word in the sentence in which *Y* represents the long *I* sound. Then ask that child to invite a classmate to circle the words in the sentence in which *Y* stands for the long *E* sound. Continue in this manner for the remaining sentences. You may also wish to use different colors of chalk to help the children discriminate between those words with the long *E* sound and those with the long *I* sound.

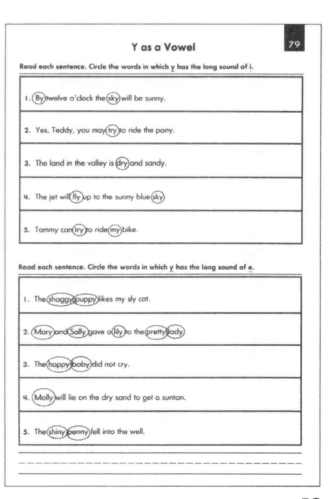

Lesson 28
W as a Vowel   (page 80)

Objective   The child will apply the Vowel *W* Rule to identify the sound of *W* in words.

Vowel *W* Rule: When *W* comes at the end of a word or syllable, it stands for a vowel sound, as in the word *snow*.

Review

Writing   Place picture flashcards of the following words on the chalkboard ledge or in a pocket chart: *wagon, windmill, yo-yo, web*. (These picture flashcards may be prepared by you ahead of time, or you may wish to use simple sketches on the chalkboard.) Invite the children to say the name of each picture. Encourage a volunteer to write the name of each picture and to identify the beginning sound heard in each word. (This may be done at the chalkboard by individual children, or by all the children at their desks using paper and pencils.) Challenge the children to give another word that starts with the same sound as each of the picture words. Acknowledge the children's responses, providing help with spelling as it is needed.

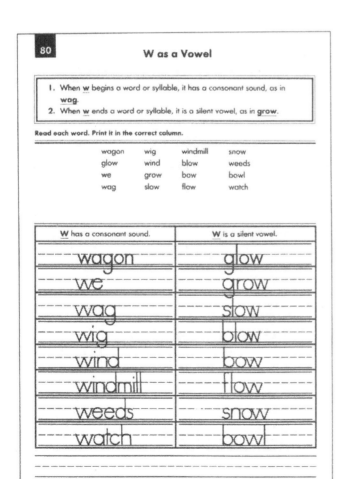

Teaching Ideas

Listening   Write the following words on the chalkboard: *snow, bow, tow, crow, slow, row, low*. Invite the children to read each word, listening for the vowel sound heard in each. As the children identify the vowel sound, explain that when *W* is at the end of a one-part word—or one-syllable word—it becomes a silent vowel. In the word *snow*, for example, *W* is the silent vowel while the vowel sound being heard is long *O*.

List the following words on the chalkboard: *snowman, window, willow, mowing*. For each word, have a volunteer divide the word into syllables by drawing a diagonal line between the syllables. Ask the child to read the word, identify the vowel sound heard in each syllable, and circle the silent *W* in each word. Encourage children to explain why the *W* is a silent vowel.

Writing   Write the following words on the chalkboard or write each word on a long strip of paper: *blow, bow, flow, own, show, tow, crow, grow, row, slow, low, glow, mow*. Say each word, asking the children to repeat the words after you. Divide the children into pairs, assign each pair one of the words, and have each pair create a sentence using the assigned word. Encourage the children to print their sentences on the strips of paper or on their own paper. (Offer assistance with punctuation and spelling as needed.) Invite the children to read their sentences aloud to the class.

Art   Allowing the children to remain in pairs, challenge them to illustrate their sentences on large pieces of newsprint or construction paper. (The children might use crayon, markers, colored chalk, or paint to illustrate their sentences.) Display the sentences with the illustrations in the classroom.

Extension

Writing   Write the following sentences on the chalkboard or on strips of paper.

1. *My bike tows your yellow wagon.*
2. *The weak crow ate a bowl of grain.*
3. *Wilma has a cute bow in her wig.*
4. *The wind will blow snow on the snowman.*
5. *Walter is mowing the grass.*
6. *Dad shut the row of windows.*

Ask the child to read the first sentence and to underline the words in which *W* stands for a vowel sound. Continue by inviting the child to circle the word in the first sentence in which *W* is a consonant. Challenge the child to apply the Vowel *W* Rule. Continue in this manner with the remaining sentences. (If you feel that it is unnecessary for the child to repeat the Vowel *W* Rule each time, you may wish to ask for it only as reinforcement if the child has difficulty identifying the words with vowel *W*.)

Lesson 29
Consonant Digraphs
TH and *WH* (pages 81–83)

Objective The child will identify the digraphs *th* and *wh* in isolation and within words.

A consonant digraph consists of two consonants that together represent a new sound.

Review

Speaking To review long and short vowel sounds, write the following words on the chalkboard, and have the children read and listen for the vowel sound in each word.

put	*cube*	*men*	*kite*
kick	*tip*	*bat*	*neat*
rose	*tale*	*hop*	*my*

As the children identify the vowel sound in each word, challenge them to state, in their own words, the appropriate Vowel Rule. (You may wish to list the rules on the board as the children say them.)

Teaching Ideas

Speaking Write the following words in two rows on the chalkboard: *this, that, those, these; think, thorn, thank, thin.* Say each group of words, inviting the children to repeat each word after you. Encourage the children to compare the sound of *th* in the first group of words with the sound of *th* in the second group of words. Explain to the children that the digraph *th* can have either a soft sound or a hard sound. Invite the children to say the words again. Encourage them to be aware of the vibration that occurs between their tongues and teeth as they pronounce the soft sound of *th* in the words in the first group. Invite the children to pronounce the words in the second group and ask if they feel the same vibration when they are pronouncing the hard sound of *th*.

Writing Have each child write the following words on a piece of paper (you may also wish to list them on the chalkboard): *thumb, three, throne, thin, thick, this, father, mother.* Ask the children to read each word and to trace the *th* digraph in each of the words with red pencil or crayon.

Write the following words on the chalkboard: *whale, wheat, wheel, whip, whisper, whisker, white, whisk.* Invite the children to repeat each word after you. For each word, challenge a volunteer to identify the digraph by circling it. (You may wish to allow those children who are reluctant to partici-

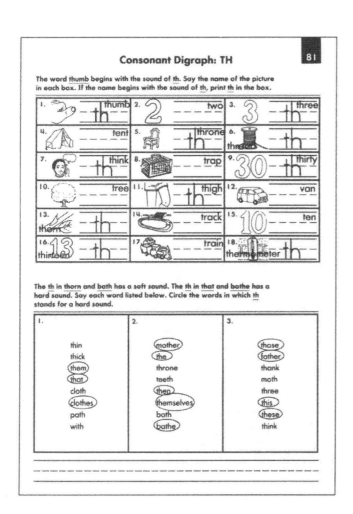

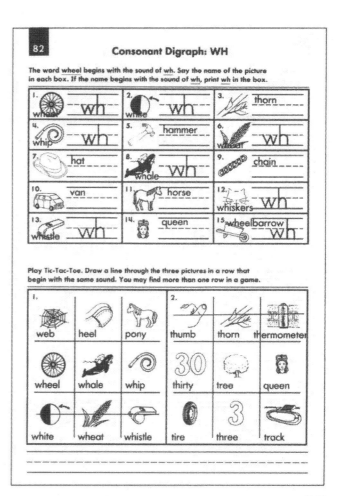

pate to choose the color of chalk they'd prefer to use on the chalkboard.) Stress that *wh* is the digraph in each word.

Art Have the children fold pieces of newsprint or construction paper into four squares. Then have the children write a *th* or *wh* word in the corner of each square. (Words may be provided on the chalkboard if the children have difficulty thinking of appropriate words.) Ask the children to draw a picture to illustrate the word in each square.

Reteaching

Change-It Game Play the Change-It Game by writing the following words on the chalkboard or on small pieces of tagboard: *mink, rose, reel, tip, tale, men, bat, corn, kite, neat, my.* Challenge the child to make a new word by changing the beginning consonant of each word to *th* or *wh.* Allow the child to experiment until an actual word is discovered. Record the new words. Encourage the child to use each of the new words in a sentence.

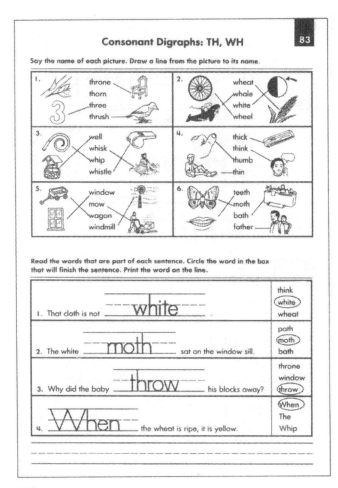

Lesson 30

Consonant Digraphs

SH and CH (pages 84–87)

Objective The child will identify the digraphs *sh* and *ch* in isolation and within words.

Review

You may wish to review consonant digraphs *th* and *wh* by inviting the children to identify the digraph in each of the following words: *these, think, why, teeth, which, thin, thunder, where, this, wheel, thick, whisper.*

Teaching Ideas

Listening Write the following words on the chalkboard: *chain, chair, cherries, sheep, shirt, shoe.* Read the words aloud, having the children repeat the words after you. You may wish to remind the children that a consonant digraph is composed of two consonants that represent a new sound. Point out that the digraph heard in each of these words is either *sh* or *ch.* In turn, invite volunteers to trace, either with a finger or with chalk, the digraph in each word while repeating the sound of the digraph.

List the following words on the chalkboard: *match, watch, beach, wish, brush, fish.* Read the words aloud, again

having the children repeat each word after you. Encourage the children to identify the consonant digraph heard at the end of each of these words, reminding them that the digraph will be either *sh* or *ch.* Invite the children to trace the digraphs in each word, repeating the sound of each digraph. You may then wish to have the children use each of the words listed on the chalkboard in a sentence.

Writing Write the following sentences on the chalkboard.

1. *Mother got peaches at the store.*
2. *Why do you like chocolate milk shakes?*
3. *When do you wish to go to the cheese store?*
4. *Which chipmunk ate the chestnuts?*
5. *I wish I had a chicken's wishbone.*

In turn, have volunteers read each sentence, name the words in each sentence that have a consonant digraph, and underline the digraph in each of these words.

Extension

Writing Place picture flashcards of the following words on the chalkboard ledge: *chain, peach, dishes, brush, sheep, mouth, thermometer, whale, wheel.* (These picture flashcards may be prepared by you prior to the lesson, or by the

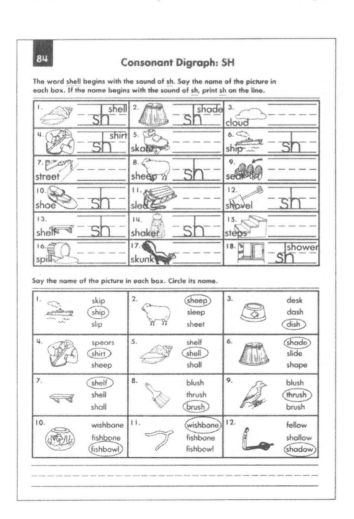

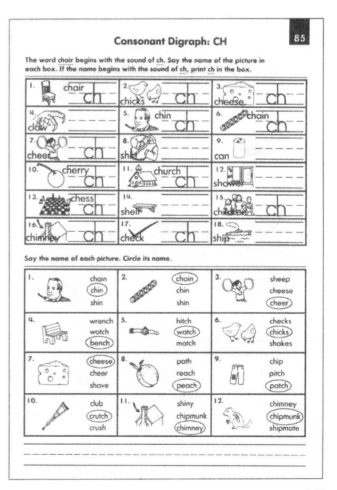

child as part of the lesson, using pictures from magazines. Save the pictures for future use.) Above each picture flash-card, draw three-way split boxes similar to the following.

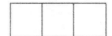

Invite the child to name each picture and to write the name of the picture above its respective box. (You may prefer to write the names yourself.) Encourage the child to identify the digraph heard in each word, and to locate the position of the digraph in the word as the beginning, the middle, or the end. Have the child print the digraph in the appropriate box.

Lesson 31
Hard and Soft Sounds of C (pages 88–89)

Objective The child will distinguish between the hard and soft sounds of *C*.

Soft C Rule: When *C* is followed by *E, I,* or *Y,* it usually represents a soft *S* sound.

Teaching Ideas

Listening Write the following columns of words on the chalkboard.

came	cent
cub	fence
cup	city
cone	pencil
candy	face

Read each word aloud, encouraging the children to listen for the sound of letter *C* in each word. Explain to the children that in the first column of words, the letter *C* represents the *K* sound, which is the hard sound of *C*. Repeat the words in the first column, inviting the children to repeat them after you. Ask the children to listen for the hard *C* sound. Continue by explaining that in the second column of words, the letter *C* represents the *S* sound, which is the soft sound of *C*. Repeat the words in the second column, inviting the children to say them after you. Encourage the children to listen for the soft sound of *C* in each word. Finally, ask the children to circle the vowel that follows the letter *C* in each word. Review with the children the application of the Soft *C* Rule to the words in the second column. You may then wish to have the children state the Soft *C* Rule in their own words.

Speaking Write the following sentences on the chalkboard.

1. *The little boy bruised his face.*
2. *I enjoy a big city.*
3. *This cake tastes good.*
4. *Some of this candy is old.*
5. *Dad likes my toy race car.*

Have a volunteer read each sentence and encourage the rest of the children to listen for the word that contains the hard or soft *C* sound. For the first sentence, point out that the word *face* contains soft *C*. Stress that the *C* is soft because it is followed by an *E*. Continue with the remaining sentences following the same procedure.

Writing Ask the children to fold a piece of paper in half vertically. Ask them to write *Soft C* at the top of one half and *Hard C* at the top of the other half. Challenge the children to list as many words as possible for each column. Invite the children to read their lists while you record their responses on the chalkboard. Encourage the children to compare the responses of their classmates to their own lists.

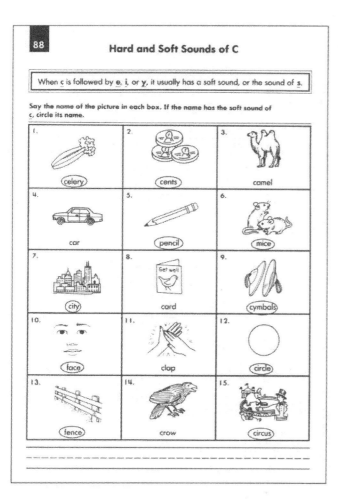

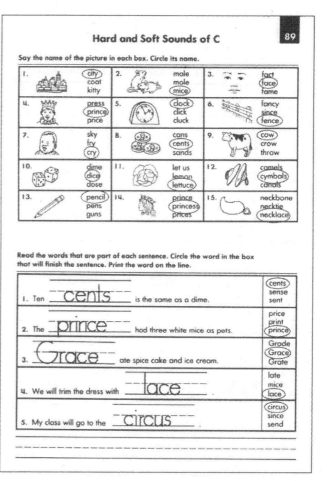

Lesson 32
Hard and Soft Sounds of G (pages 90–92)

Objective The child will distinguish between the hard and soft sounds of *G*.

Soft *G* Rule: When *G* is followed by *E, I,* or *Y*, the *G* usually represents a soft *J* sound.

Review

Speaking To review the hard and soft sounds of *C*, print the following words on the chalkboard.

cot   fence   city   circle
dice   circus   fancy   race
cup   cent   face   cans

In turn, invite volunteers to read each word, telling whether the *C* has a hard or soft sound. Challenge the children to state, in their own words, the rule that applies to the soft *C* words.

Teaching Ideas

Listening Write the following two columns of words on the chalkboard: *gave, gun, got, grab, grow; cage, gym, gem, giant, bridge.* Read each word aloud, encouraging the children to listen for the sound of *G* in each. Explain to the children that in the first column of words, the letter *G* represents the hard sound of *G*, as heard in the word *go*. Say the words in the first column again. Have the children repeat the words after you, emphasizing the hard sound of *G* in each word. Continue by explaining to the children that in the second column of words, the letter *G* represents the *J* sound, which is the soft sound of *G*. Again, encourage the children to repeat the words in the second column, emphasizing the soft *G* sound in each word. To reinforce the Soft *G* Rule, ask the children to identify the vowel that follows the letter *G* in each of the words in the second column. Remind the children that when *G* is followed by *E, I,* or *Y*, the letter *G* usually represents the *J* sound, which is the soft sound of *G*. You may then wish to ask the children to think of more words that have soft or hard *G*. Add their suggestions to the appropriate column on the chalkboard.

Writing Write the following words on the chalkboard: *giraffe, gate, gym, game, glass, giant, gingerbread, gum, frog, cage, wig, wagon.* Divide the children into small groups. (Groups of two or three would be most manageable.) Assign to each group one of the *G* words listed on the chalkboard. Challenge the children to create a sentence using the word their group has been assigned. Ask the children to write their group's sentence on precut strips of paper or on their own paper, highlighting the *G* word. (This may be done by using a brightly colored crayon or marker.) When the sentences are completed, have each group read their sentence, identify the

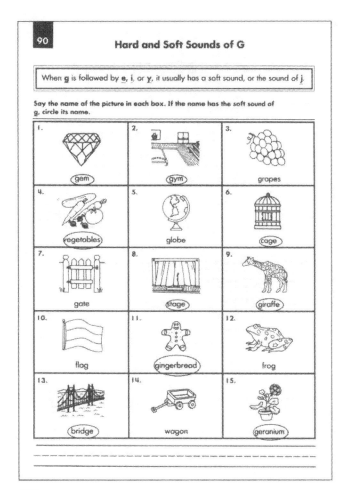

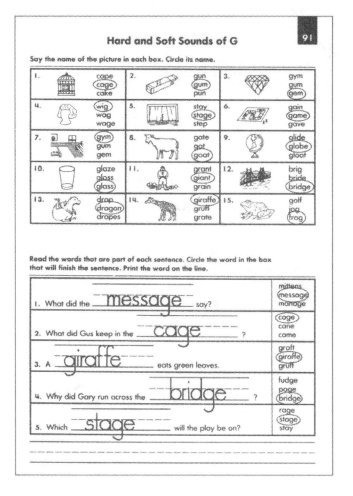

G word, and explain whether the *G* word has the soft or hard sound of *G*.

Extension

Writing Write the following headings on the chalkboard: *Soft G, Hard G.* Say the following words.

age	*gun*	*page*	*cage*	*wig*	*glass*
frog	*gym*	*goat*	*game*	*giant*	*stage*
bridge	*edge*	*gem*	*ginger*	*message*	

Encourage the child to listen for the *G* sound in each word. Challenge the child to write the word in the appropriate column on the chalkboard. (Offer assistance with spelling if necessary.) Invite the child to circle the letter that follows the letter *G* in each word. Review the Soft *G* Rule with the child.

Family Involvement Activity Duplicate the Family Letter on page 105 of this Teacher's Edition. Send it home with the children.

---

92   **Soft Sounds of C and G**

Read each sentence. Underline the words in which g has a soft sound. Then circle the words in which c has a soft sound.

1. It is nice to sit by a fireplace.

2. The mice have lots of space in their nest.

3. A huge globe hung from the ceiling.

4. The bandits held up the stagecoach.

5. His father let him keep the change.

6. They will have ice cream and fruit juice at the dance.

7. Kim came with a strange message.

8. Soap helps us to get rid of germs.

9. Use your pencil to print your name and age on this tag.

10. Grace will lead the class in a pledge to the flag.

Unit 7   Vowels with *R*

Lesson 33
AR   (pages 93–94)

Objective   The child will associate the letters *ar* with the sound the letters usually represent.

Teaching Ideas

Listening   Write the word *star* on the chalkboard. Say the word aloud, inviting the children to repeat the word after you. Underline the *ar* in *star*. Explain to the children that when *A* and *R* are sounded together, they make a new vowel sound, as in the word *star*. Continue by saying the following words: *arm, star, car, yarn, art, farm, yard*. Encourage the children to repeat each word after you, listening for the *ar* vowel sound.

Speaking   Write the following words on the chalkboard.

car	*art*	*barn*	*arm*
bar	*cart*	*yarn*	*harm*
jar	*tart*	*darn*	*farm*
arch	*charm*	*Carl*	*start*
scar	*march*	*garden*	*far*

In turn, invite volunteers to point to a word, read it aloud, and underline the *ar* letters. Finally, challenge the child to use the word in a sentence.

Art   Invite the children to make an *ar* vowel collage. Give each child a piece of construction paper or tagboard. Encourage the children to find pictures of things with names that have the *ar* vowel sound in magazines. (You may wish to refer the children to the words listed in the Speaking portion of the lesson if they find it difficult to think of *ar* words.) Ask the children to cut out the pictures and paste them on construction paper, producing a collage by overlapping the pictures. Then display the collages within the classroom.

Reteaching

Art   Invite the child to make a set of *ar* word cards. Provide the child with small squares of tagboard or construction paper. Write the following list of words on the chalkboard: *car, barn, garden, jar, yarn, star, cart, arm, dart*. Encourage the child to draw a picture of each object listed on one of the squares. Ask the child to write the word that represents the picture at the top of the square, underlining the *ar* vowel in each word. Challenge the child to think of additional *ar* vowel words to make into word cards.

Lesson 34

OR (pages 95–96)

Objective The child will identify the sound of *or* appearing in isolation or in words.

Review

Listening To review words that contain the *ar* sound, write the following words on the chalkboard: *bark, harm, tar, cart, car, farm, card, park, star, jar.* Invite the children to say each word and circle the letters that make the *ar* sound.

Erase some of the words, leaving only the words *bark, harm,* and *tar* on the chalkboard. Encourage the children to create new words by substituting a different consonant for the first letter or the last letter of each word. Write these new words on the chalkboard as they are suggested. For example, *harm* can be changed to *hard* or *farm.*

Teaching Ideas

Speaking Display prepared picture flashcards for the following *or* words on the chalkboard ledge: *horn, born, storm, corn.* Write the name of each picture on the chalkboard above the appropriate picture flashcard. Encourage the children to repeat each word after you, listening for the *or* sound. Point out that together *O* and *R* have formed a new sound.

Write the following words on the chalkboard: *word, work, world, worst.* Encourage the children to repeat each word and to identify the sound that *or* makes. Point out that when a word or a syllable begins with *WOR*, it usually has a *ur* sound.

Around-the-World Game Prepare a set of word cards for *or* words that include words such as the following: *short, morning, scorch, storm, forty.* (You may wish to include the *ar* words from the previous lesson.) Direct the children to stand in a line one behind the other. Show a word card to the child at the front of the line and challenge the child to identify the vowel sound. Continue with each child in the line, distributing the word card to each child responding correctly. Continue the game until all the word cards have been distributed. Have the child holding the most word cards assume the role of the "teacher" in a subsequent game.

Listening Write the following sentences and word pairs on the chalkboard.

1. A flying bird with long legs and a long beak is a _____ . (stork/start)
2. The baby was _____ last week. (born/barn)
3. My _____ is to the left of my plate. (fork/fort)
4. Shawn likes to honk the _____ . (harp/horn)
5. I am too _____ to reach the jar. (star/short)

Have the children fill in the blank spaces with the correct words. To encourage those who are having trouble identifying correct answers, point out differences between the word pairs.

OR 95

The word *horn* has the sound of *or*. Say the name of the picture in each box. Print *or* on the line in the box if you hear the sound of *or*.

1. horn	2. fork	3. cart
4. corn	5. jar	6. porch
7. barn	8. star	9. stork
10. horse	11. thorn	12. car
13. torch	14. forty	15. porcupine

Say the name of the picture in each box. Circle its name.

1. (corn) car core	2. (car) core	3. harm (horn) hard
4. far (fork) fort	5. (yarn) yard jar	6. cork (core) corn
7. (torch) arch porch	8. park torch (porch)	9. (ford) fork fort
10. stare (star) store	11. star (store) store	12. (stork) storm starch
13. harm (horn) horse	14. (thorn) throne tart	15. fork fifty (forty)

---

96 **OR**

Read the words that are part of each rhyme. Choose the word from the box that will finish the rhyme. Print the word on the line.

1. Oh! What a chore / To go to the —,	store	score / store / snore
2. The men are apt to scorch / The oak tree with that —.	torch	scorch / porch / torch
3. We will add up the score / Before we play some —.	more	more / tore / sore
4. His pants were torn / By the —.	thorn	torch / corn / thorn
5. Down the street went little Cindy. / Off went her hat, since it was —.	windy	witty / windy / whine

Read the words that are part of each sentence. Finish the sentence by writing the words from the box in the correct order on the line.

1. Tom likes to	eat sweet corn .	eat / corn / sweet
2. Sue can play	the horn well .	horn / well / the
3. May I sit on	your porch swing ?	porch / swing / your
4. You can get horned toads at	the pet store .	store / pet / the
5. Did Mom forbid you to play	on the shore ?	shore / on / the

---

63

Lesson 35
IR, UR, and ER (pages 97–100)

Objective   The child will identify the sound of *ir*, *ur*, and *er* appearing in isolation or in words.

Review

Listening   To practice auditory discrimination between the soft *C* and the soft *G* sounds, encourage the children to repeat each of the following words after you: *ceiling, cymbals, fancy, age, giraffe, gym, strange, icing, mice, city, page, cent, stage, fence, giant*. Ask the children to identify the soft *C* or the soft *G* sound in each word. You may wish to use prepared word cards of soft *C* and soft *G* words.

Teaching Ideas

Art   Place prepared picture flashcards for *girl, ladder,* and *nurse* on the chalkboard ledge, writing *ir, er,* and *ur* above the appropriate picture flashcards.

Help the children create additional picture flashcards for the *ir, ur,* and *er* sounds. For example, after the children draw or paste a picture of a *purse* on one side of a tagboard card, you can write the word *nurse* on the chalkboard. Have the children

identify the *ur* sound made by the letters *ur*, and ask them to write the letters *ur* on the other side of the picture flashcard. (Collect these picture flashcards for use in the following activity.)

Listening   Invite the children to display some of the picture flashcards they made as part of the last activity. Encourage the other children to identify the picture and the *ur* sound in each name.

Writing   Write the following sentences on the chalkboard or on large chart paper.

1. *A spiderweb was in the fir tree.*
2. *Miss Burns lost her purse in church.*
3. *Did the wrestler hurt his arm?*
4. *The little bird has a dirty worm.*
5. *The girl was thirsty after working so hard.*

Encourage the children to read each sentence and to circle the *ir, ur,* and *er* words. Have the children copy the words in the sentences that have these sounds on sheets of paper.

Memory Game   Play the following variation of a classic memory game to develop both memory and phonics skills. Ask a child to complete the following sentence with a word that has the sound of *ir, ur,* or *er*: *I went on a trip and I took a _____* . Invite another volunteer to repeat the sentence, adding another item that has one of the targeted sounds. Point out that each item must be repeated in the correct

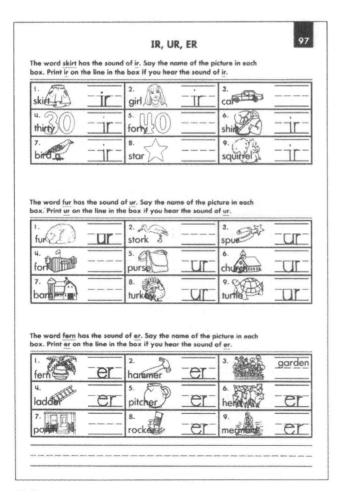

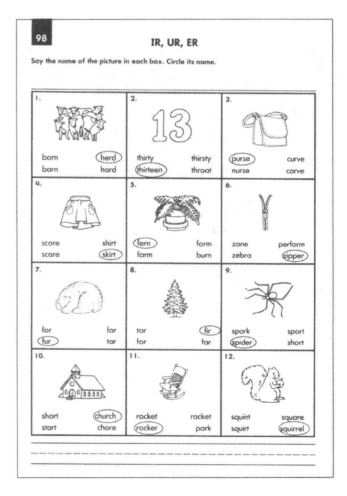

sequence. Continue the game until the items are repeated out of sequence or an item is included that does not begin with any of the targeted sounds.

Reteaching

Listening   Have the child use prepared picture flash-cards for words with names that have a vowel plus *R*. As the child identifies each picture name, ask which vowel sound is heard.

Unit 8 Suffixes; Contractions

Lesson 36
Suffixes *S* and *ES* (pages 101–102)

Objective   The child will form plural words by adding *s* and *es* to base words.

If a word ends in *x, ss, sh, ch,* or *z,* we usually add *es* to form the plural.

Review

Listening   To practice recognition of the *ar, or, ir,* and *ur* sounds, display the following picture flashcards on the chalkboard ledge: *car, girls, horn, nurse, star, turkey, horse.* As the children identify each picture, write the word on the chalkboard above each picture flashcard. (Keep the words on the chalkboard for the following activity.)

Writing   Refer to the words on the chalkboard and encourage the children to write each word on a sheet of paper and to use each word in a sentence.

Teaching Ideas

Speaking   Write the following words on the chalkboard: *hat, dog, car, key, bird, camp.* Explain to the children that adding an *s* to each word will make it plural, or more than one. Encourage the children to read each word aloud and have a volunteer write an *s* beside each word on the chalkboard. Once the plural words are formed, encourage the children to read each one with you. (Keep the words on the chalkboard for the following activity.)

Listening   Using the words from the previous activity, invite volunteers to underline a base word on the chalkboard. Ask the children to explain the difference between *hat* and *hats*. Point out that when *s* is added to a base word to refer to more than one thing, the word becomes a plural word.

Write the following words on the chalkboard and encourage the children to repeat each word: *buzz, peach, box, dress, dish.* Provide the following spelling tip: *When a base word ends in* x, z, ss, ch, *or* sh, *we usually add* es *to make that word plural.* Add the suffix *es* to each word to create the plurals.

Explain that *es* is heard as a syllable, but that *s* alone is not. Invite the children to repeat the plural words on the chalkboard. Have them clap to indicate each syllable.

Writing   Stack word cards for the following words: *brush, peach, key, box, bird, latch, dress.* Invite the children to select a word card, to identify the word, and to tell whether *s* or *es* is added to form the plural of that word. For example, *es* is added to the word *brush* to create its plural. Write the plural words on the chalkboard so the children can see the correct spelling. Encourage the children to write the plural words that are on the chalkboard on sheets of paper.

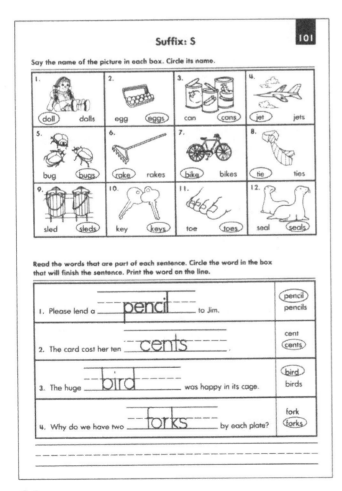

Lesson 37
Suffix *ES* After *Y*   (pages 103–104)

Objective   The child will form plural words by adding *es* to base words ending in *y*.

If a word ends in *Y*, we usually change the *Y* to *I* and add *es* to form the plural.

Review

Writing   To review *s* and *es* suffixes, write the following words on the chalkboard and invite the children to make them plural: *box, branch, bug, buzz, miss, star, tax, wish, bunch, can, bush, bench, bus, mop, glass, fox, pet.* When the plural for each word has been formed, encourage the children to create a picture representation for each word.

Teaching Ideas

Visual Discrimination   Write the following words on the chalkboard: *pony, daisy, puppy, penny, gypsy, baby.* Invite the children to circle the last letter of each word. Point out the *E* sound made by the letter *Y*. Provide the following spelling tip: *If a word ends in a consonant plus* Y, *we usually change the* Y *to* I *and add* es *to form the plural of the word.*

Write *pony* on the chalkboard and challenge a volunteer to use the spelling tip to form the plural of the word. Follow the same procedure for each word, asking the children to apply the spelling tip and to write the plural spelling of each word.

Writing   Write the following plural words on the chalkboard: *berries, cities, parties, flies, ponies, puppies, cherries, ladies, daisies.* Ask the children to write the base word for each plural on a sheet of paper.

Home-Run Game   Designate the four corners of the room as the bases for the game. Divide the children into two teams. Stack word cards for singular and plural words found in this lesson and in Lesson 36. (You may wish to save these cards to continue the game in Lesson 38.) Choose a team to be "up to bat." Ask the first child on that team to choose a card, to read the word, and to use the word in a sentence. Direct the child who responds correctly to move ahead one base. (As in baseball, the progress of one player moves the previous players forward as well.) If a player misses a word or uses it incorrectly, call an "out." After three "outs," have the other team come "up to bat." Continue the game for nine innings or until the cards are all used. Determine the winning team by the number of "runs" each team accumulates.

Extension

Writing   Prepare plural word cards and display them on the chalkboard ledge. Encourage the child to choose five words and to write these words in sentences.

Suffix: ES After Y | 103

If a word that ends in y is preceded by a consonant, we usually change the y to i and add **es** to form the plural.

Print the plural for each word on the line.

1. pony	ponies	2. lily	lilies
3. fly	flies	4. baby	babies
5. sky	skies	6. buggy	buggies
7. story	stories	8. city	cities
9. penny	pennies	10. party	parties

Read the words that are part of each sentence. Finish the sentence with the plural form of the word in the box. Print the plural form on the line.

1. Please, read us some __stories__ .	story
2. Some cities have big __parks__ .	park
3. We had bowls of fresh __berries__ at the party.	berry
4. Misty is the mother of six __puppies__ .	puppy
5. The garden is full of daisies and __lilies__ .	lily

---

104 | Suffixes: S, ES, IES

Print the plural form of each word on the line.

1. lady	ladies	2. truck	trucks
3. berry	berries	4. dress	dresses
5. pony	ponies	6. puppy	puppies
7. jet	jets	8. fox	foxes
9. dish	dishes	10. beach	beaches

Read the words that are part of each sentence. Finish the sentence with the plural form of the word in the box. Print the plural form on the line.

1. Five of the __girls__ went to the game on a bus.	girl
2. The puppies ate the basket of __peaches__ .	peach
3. Kate went to pick some fresh __berries__ .	berry
4. Bob needs two __boxes__ for his toys.	box
5. The children had to pay to ride the __ponies__ .	pony

Lesson 38
Suffixes *ES* and *ED* After *Y* (page 105)

Objective   The child will add suffixes *es* or *ed* to base words ending in *Y*.

If a word ends in Y preceded by a consonant, change the Y to I before adding es or ed.

Review

Speaking   To review *ar, or, ir, er,* and *ur* words, write the following words on the chalkboard: *jar, yard, hornet, morning, church, dirt, shirt, spider, thirteen, surprise, party.* Encourage the children to say each word and to identify and circle letters that make the sound of a vowel plus *R*. You might have the children use each word in a sentence.

Teaching Ideas

Listening   Write the following words on the chalkboard: *fry, spy, empty, shy, try, copy, study, carry.* Encourage the children to read the words and to identify the final *Y* sound in each. Encourage the children to note that a consonant precedes the final *Y* in these words. Have a volunteer circle the letter that comes just before the *Y* in each word. Provide the following spelling tip: *When a word ends in Y preceded by a consonant, change the Y to I before adding* es *or* ed. Use the word *fry* as an example to help the children understand the rule: *fry/fries/fried.* Add *es* and *ed* to each of the other words on the chalkboard. Ask the children to read the words and to apply the tip for adding the suffixes *es* and *ed.*

Home-Run Game   Using the words from this lesson, prepare word cards for base words and for base words with the *es* and *ed* endings. Play the Home-Run Game, as described in Lesson 37 in this unit, using these cards. As a challenge, you may wish to add the word cards used in the Home-Run Game in Lesson 37 to these cards and continue playing in the same manner.

Extension

Writing   Write the following words on the chalkboard: *copied, fried, spies, carried, dries, hurried.* Ask the child to write a sentence for each word on a sheet of paper.

Suffixes: ES and ED After Y |105|

When a word ends in a consonant plus y, change the y to i before adding es or ed.

Add the suffixes es and ed to each word. Print the new words on the lines.

cry	cries	cried
fry	fries	fried
spy	spies	spied
dry	dries	dried
try	tries	tried
deny	denies	denied
copy	copies	copied
carry	carries	carried
study	studies	studied
empty	empties	emptied
hurry	hurries	hurried

68

Lesson 39
Suffix *ED*   (pages 106–108)

Objective   The child will form and read words ending in *ed* in isolation and within sentences.

Review

Writing   To practice adding the plural suffixes *s* and *es* to words ending in *Y*, write the following words on the chalkboard: *day, key, cry, dry, say, toy, study, spy.* For each, invite a volunteer to read the word and add either *s* or *es*. Have the child explain why the ending was chosen.

As a variation, write *s* and *ed* on the chalkboard as column headings. For each word, ask a child to read the base word and to write the base word plus the suffix in the correct column.

Teaching Ideas

Listening   Point out that suffixes that are spelled the same do not always sound the same. Tell the children that the suffix *ed* sometimes sounds like *ed*, sometimes sounds like *t*, and sometimes sounds like *d*. Write *ed, t,* and *d* on the chalkboard as column headings. Encourage the children to listen carefully as you pronounce each of the following words, exaggerating the final sound: *dusted, marched, cleaned, helped, dreamed, locked, seated, painted, mailed.* Repeat each word and invite a volunteer to identify the sound heard at the end of

each word. After the child gives the correct response, write the word in the proper column and circle the *ed*. (You may point out that the part of the word that is not circled is the base word.) If a child has difficulty, you might ask the child to repeat the word after you.

Speaking   Distribute the following word cards to the children: *camped, burned, darted, fished, loaded, helped, planted, played.* For each word card, have the child show the word card to the class, read the word aloud, and identify the base word. Reinforce a correct response by having the child ask a classmate to use the word in a sentence.

Reading   Write the following sentences on the chalkboard.

1. *We asked Dad for a ride to the game.*
2. *His car failed to start.*
3. *Dad raised the hood of the car.*
4. *He looked at the motor.*
5. *We helped by keeping quiet as Dad worked.*
6. *Dad dusted the wires and squirted some oil.*
7. *Then Dad smiled and closed the hood.*
8. *The car was fixed.*

For each, have a volunteer read the sentence and identify the words ending with the suffix *ed* by underlining them. Then ask the child to circle the base word and to give the sound of the *ed* suffix. (If you decide to do the following Extension exercise, keep these sentences from the chalkboard.)

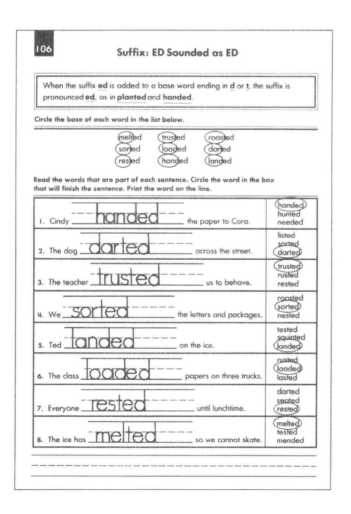

106   Suffix: ED Sounded as ED

When the suffix **ed** is added to a base word ending in **d** or **t**, the suffix is pronounced **ed**, as in **planted** and **handed**.

Circle the base of each word in the list below.

(melt)ed   (trust)ed   (roast)ed
(sort)ed   (load)ed   (dart)ed
(rest)ed   (hand)ed   (land)ed

Read the words that are part of each sentence. Circle the word in the box that will finish the sentence. Print the word on the line.

1. Cindy __handed__ the paper to Cora.   (handed) / hunted / needed
2. The dog __darted__ across the street.   listed / sorted / (darted)
3. The teacher __trusted__ us to behave.   (trusted) / rusted / rested
4. We __sorted__ the letters and packages.   roasted / (sorted) / nested
5. Ted __landed__ on the ice.   tested / squinted / (landed)
6. The class __loaded__ papers on three trucks.   rusted / (loaded) / lasted
7. Everyone __rested__ until lunchtime.   darted / seated / (rested)
8. The ice has __melted__ so we cannot skate.   (melted) / tested / mended

107   Suffix: ED Sounded as T

When the suffix **ed** is added to a base word that does not end in **d** or **t**, the suffix is sometimes pronounced **t**, as in **jumped**.

Draw a ring around the base of each word in the list below.

(leap)ed   (cross)ed   (ask)ed
(puff)ed   (help)ed   (rush)ed
(tick)ed   (fix)ed   (pack)ed

Read the words that are part of each sentence. Circle the word in the box that will finish the sentence. Print the word on the line.

1. Dad __rushed__ to catch the bus.   crushed / (rushed) / crushed
2. He __leaped__ over the fence and ran fast.   (leaped) / peeped / heaped
3. Tommy __asked__ his mother for some fruit.   mixed / boxed / (asked)
4. Jane __packed__ a large picnic lunch.   backed / (packed) / picked
5. Who __fixed__ the dessert for the picnic?   waxed / (fixed) / taxed
6. Dick huffed and __puffed__ to lift the big box.   pasted / gifted / (puffed)
7. When we __crossed__ the river, the boat leaked.   (crossed) / pressed / dressed
8. We all __helped__ to clean up before we left.   handed / (helped) / hinted

Extension

Sequencing Encourage the child to read silently through the eight sentences again, this time concentrating on the story they tell. Have the child draw a series of two or three pictures for a comic strip illustration of the story. You may want to have the child label the pictures with the appropriate sentences.

Another approach would be to write the story on sentence strips, with sentences 1 and 2 on one strip, 3 and 4 on a second strip, 5 and 6 on a third strip, and 7 and 8 on a fourth strip. Do not number the strips. Shuffle the strips and have the child organize them in the correct sequence.

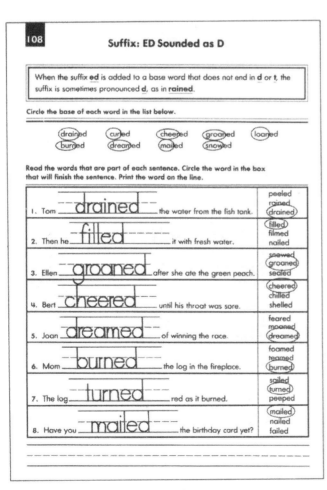

Lesson 40
Suffix *ING* (page 109)

Objective   The child will form and read words ending in *ing*.

Review

Reading   To review the consonant digraphs *th, wh, sh,* and *ch,* write the following sentences on the chalkboard.
1. *My mother took the peaches into the kitchen.*
2. *There is a moth in the dish.*
3. *Tanya has a patch on her shorts.*
4. *Which chimp chewed on those boxes?*

For each, invite a volunteer to read the sentence and to circle the words containing a digraph.

Teaching Ideas

Speaking   To introduce the suffix *ing,* write the following sentence on the chalkboard: *The monkey will jump when he sees that the clown is jumping.* Read the sentence aloud and circle the words *jump* and *jumping.* Have the children identify the base word. Reinforce the correct response by pointing out that the letters *ing* form a suffix, or a syllable added to the end of a base word to make a new word. Explain that many new words are formed by adding the suffix *ing* to base words.

Provide additional practice by writing the following words on the chalkboard: *eat, cry, wink, swing.* In turn, invite volunteers to read each word and to create a new word by copying the word on the chalkboard and adding *ing.* Have each child read the new word. Challenge the children to create sentences using the new pairs of words in place of *jump* and *jumping* (for example: *The monkey will eat when he sees that the clown is eating.*).

Writing   Write the following words and incomplete sentences on the chalkboard.

help   pay   load   melt   fix
1. *Mom is _____ the bills.*
2. *Su-Han is _____ his bike.*
3. *My sister is _____ my father.*
4. *The men are _____ boxes into the truck.*
5. *The snowman is _____ in the sun.*

Challenge a volunteer to complete the first sentence by selecting a word from the list and adding *ing* to it. Then ask the child to write the missing word on the line and to read the sentence. Proceed in the same manner for the remaining sentences. If you feel the children would benefit from independent work, you might have them write the completed sentences on their own sheets of paper. Conclude the activity by filling in each sentence on the chalkboard so the children can check their answers.

Extension

Writing   Challenge the child to make up sentences like the ones in the Speaking activity, in which both the base word and the base word with the *ing* ending added are used. You might want to provide samples.

Suffix: ING   109

Read the words that are part of each sentence. Finish the sentence by adding **ing** to one of the base words in the box. Print the new word on the line.

1.	Are you going __fishing__ with your dad?	fish / wish / fuss
2.	Rosa is __gaining__ on Tim in the race.	pain / gain / braid
3.	Why are you __filling__ the pail with water?	fail / fall / fill
4.	__Roasting__ hot dogs is fun.	Rest / Roast / Fish
5.	__Hunting__ for seashells is fun, too.	Hunt / Hand / Help
6.	The plane is just __landing__ on the runway.	air / sea / land
7.	Will you be __mailing__ the letters today?	will / mail / sell
8.	The class is __renting__ a bus to go to the zoo.	make / sell / rent
9.	__Winking__ with your left eye is hard to do.	Jump / Work / Wink
10.	When it is __raining__ we have to play inside.	sail / rain / nail
11.	He is __mending__ the toy with glue.	stand / mend / spend

Lesson 41
Suffixes: Final Consonant Doubled (pages 110–111)

Objective   The child will double the consonant in short vowel words before adding *ed* or *ing*.

When a short vowel word ends in a single consonant, we usually double the consonant before adding *ed* or *ing*.

Teaching Ideas

Reading   List the following words on the chalkboard: *skip, beg, trip, hum*. Ask if the vowel sound in each word is long or short. Ask how many consonants are at the end of each word. Invite the children to watch as you add the suffixes *ed* and *ing* to each word, producing the following three columns.

skip	skipped	skipping
beg	begged	begging
trip	tripped	tripping
hum	hummed	humming

Circle the doubled consonants in the words with suffixes and explain to the children that when a short vowel word ends in a single consonant, we usually double that consonant before adding the ending *ed* or *ing*.

Suffix Game   Prepare the following word cards: *clap, fill, hum, step, pin, sail, ship, rain, jump, drop*. Divide the children into two teams. Explain that you will flash a word card; the first child in each team is to go to the chalkboard and write a new word by adding the suffix *ed* to the word on the word card. The first child to correctly write the word with the suffix will earn a point for the team. Continue the game, being sure to include all remaining children. Ask the children to add the suffix *ing* in place of the suffix *ed*.

Reteaching

Sorting   Give the child a set of word cards containing the following words: *cleaned, helping, ripped, raining, dreaming, clapping, begging, played, humming, eating*. Ask the child to sort the word cards into two piles: one for words with a short vowel sound in the base word and one for words with a long vowel sound in the base word. Have the child compile two lists of base words, one for each pile. Ask the child to circle the list containing base words that were changed before the suffix was added. Ask the child to explain the change that took place in the base words when the *ed* or *ing* was added to short vowel words ending in a single consonant.

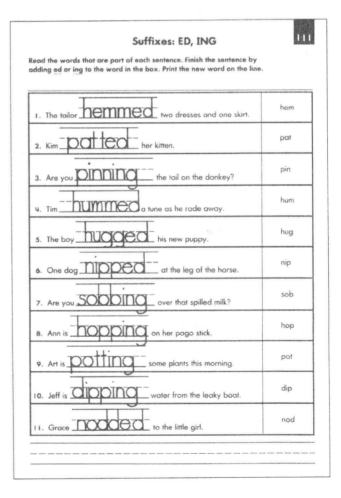

Lesson 42
Suffixes After Silent *E* (pages 112–113)

Objective The child will drop the *e* from words ending in silent *e* before adding the suffixes *ed* and *ing*.

When a word ends with a silent *e*, we usually drop the *e* from the base word before adding *ed* or *ing*.

Review

Reading To practice recognition of words with suffixes, display the following word cards: *cities, horses, wishes, chopped, fixed, mailing.* For each, invite a volunteer to read the word and to identify the base word and the suffix ending. Encourage children to tell whether the base word was changed before the suffix was added.

Teaching Ideas

Speaking You might introduce the rule about suffixes after silent *e* by briefly reviewing silent *e* words. List the following words on the chalkboard: *bake, run, beg, hope, hop, like, save, use.* Challenge a child to come forward and erase any word that does not have a long vowel sound. For each of the remaining words, have a child read the word, tell the letter that ends the word, and tell if the letter can be heard. Acknowledge any child who offers Long Vowel Rule 1 as an explanation for the silent *e*.

Write the following sets of words on the chalkboard: *bake/baked/baking, hope/hoped/hoping, like/liked/liking, save/saved/saving, use/used/using.* For each set, ask a volunteer to explain how the base word changed when *ed* and *ing*, respectively, were added. Encourage the children to say in their own words the rule for dropping silent *e* before adding *ed* or *ing*.

Suffix Game For additional practice in distinguishing when to drop the silent *e*, play the Suffix Game described in Lesson 41 in this unit. You might use the following words: *age, rain, pile, paste, tape, wink, joke, peel, pave, paint, trace, smile.*

Writing Write the following sentences on the chalkboard.

1. *Mark (like) his birthday present.*
2. *The baby (play) in the yard.*
3. *Grandma is (bake) Mark a birthday cake.*
4. *The dog (beg) for a bone.*
5. *Nancy is (hem) her skirt.*

In turn, invite volunteers to come forward and complete each sentence by adding the suffixes *ed* or *ing* to the base word in parentheses. You may want to draw attention to the fact that for each sentence only one of the two prefixes will be appropriate.

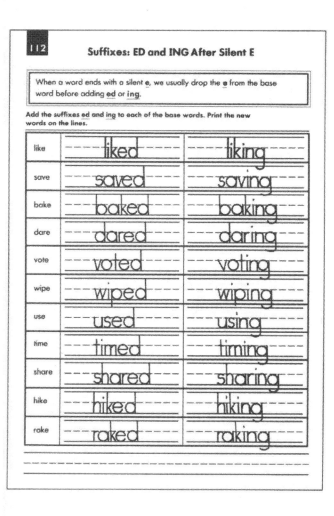

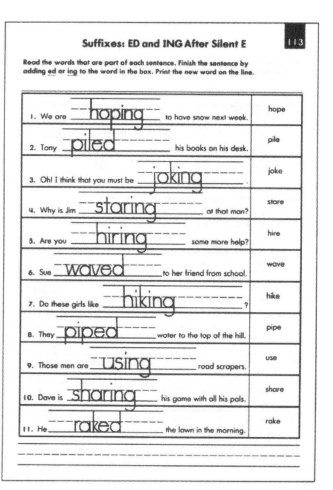

73

Lesson 43
Suffixes *FUL* and *LESS* (page 114)

Objective   The child will add the suffixes *ful* and *less* to base words and will read the newly formed words in isolation and within sentences.

Review

Writing To provide practice in adding *s* and *es* to base words, write the following incomplete sentences on the chalkboard.

1. *Jim broke two branch _____ off the tree.*
2. *Tad put three box _____ on the chair.*
3. *Did you see the five dog _____ in the yard?*
4. *Mom sewed two dress _____ for Mia.*
5. *Please put your game _____ away.*

For each, ask a volunteer to complete the base word by adding *s* or *es* and to read the completed sentence. You might review the distinction between each base word and its plural meaning.

Teaching Ideas

Speaking   Write the words *painful* and *painless* as column headings on the chalkboard. Circle the suffixes *ful* and *less* and point out that both suffixes have been added to the base word *pain*. Explain that the suffix *ful* means *full of*, while the suffix *less* means *without*. Ask a volunteer to apply these definitions to explain the meanings of *painful* and the meaning of *painless*.

Tell the children that other words can be formed by adding the suffixes *ful* and *less* to the base word. Write the words *fear*, *harm*, and *pain* on the chalkboard. Then create two new words for each by adding *ful* and *less*, writing the two new words under each base word. Invite a child to read each word and to use it in a sentence. Challenge the children to use both forms of the word in the same sentence. For example: *You should brush your teeth because it is painless to brush them, but it is painful to get a cavity.*

Reading   Write the following sentences on the chalkboard.

1. *A snake bite might be harmful.*
2. *His dog is harmless.*
3. *A day at the beach is restful.*
4. *The baby was restless.*

For each, call on a child to read the sentence, identify the word containing a suffix, and tell the meaning of the sentence.

114

Suffixes: FUL and LESS

The letters *ful* and *less* are suffixes. Draw a line under each base word listed below. Then circle each suffix.

tear(ful)	hope(less)	care(less)	pain(ful)	need(ful)
tear(less)	hope(ful)	care(ful)	pain(less)	need(less)
fear(less)	help(ful)	thank(ful)	harm(ful)	rest(less)
fear(ful)	help(less)	thank(less)	harm(less)	rest(ful)

Read each sentence. Circle the word in the box that best describes what each sentence is saying.

1. Rick did not stop before he rode his bike from the driveway into the street.	(careless) / careful
2. Luke was so happy with his birthday gifts. He gave his mother a big hug.	thankless / (thankful)
3. Mike washed the dishes and took out the trash.	helpless / (helpful)
4. The brave lady jumped into the icy river to save the baby.	(fearless) / fearful
5. The baby sobbed when he had to go to bed.	tearless / (tearful)
6. It was quiet and peaceful at the lake. Dan lay on a blanket and dreamed.	restless / (restful)
7. Kate went to see the dentist. She did not feel a thing when he pulled two of her teeth.	(painless) / painful
8. Jane would have fixed the broken teacup, but one part was missing.	(hopeless) / hopeful

---

74

Lesson 44
Suffixes *NESS* and *LY* (page 115)

Objective   The child will add the suffixes *ness* and *ly* to base words and read the newly formed words in isolation and within sentences.

Review

Reading   Have the children practice reading the following words with suffixes, identifying the base words: *tries, dressed, poked, making, humming, sharing, sleepless, thankful, useful, useless.* For each, invite a volunteer to read the word, identify the base word and the suffix, and use the word in a sentence.

Teaching Ideas

Speaking   Write the following sets of words on the chalkboard: *dark/darkness, sick/sickness, sad/sadness, slow/slowly.* For each set, ask a volunteer to read the two words and to circle the suffix in the second word. Challenge the child to use the word containing the suffix in a sentence. Encourage children to think of sentences that explain what the word means.

Reading   Write the following sentences on the chalkboard.
1. *I do not like the darkness.*
2. *She spoke softly to me.*
3. *We gladly helped rake the leaves.*
4. *Andi liked the softness of the toy animal.*
5. *Jess ran quickly to the store.*

For each, invite a volunteer to come forward, read the sentence, and identify the word with the suffix *ness* or *ly.* You might then have the child underline the base word and circle the suffix.

Extension

Writing   Challenge the child to write sentences using words with the suffixes *ness* and *ly.* You might suggest and write the following words on the chalkboard: *neat, near, sad, soft, sick.*

Suffixes: NESS, LY `115`

The letters ness and ly are suffixes. Draw a line under each base word listed below. Then circle each suffix.

| darkness | swiftly | bravely | neatness | softness |
| neatly | likeness | sadness | slowly | gladly |

Read the words that are part of each sentence. Finish the sentence by adding ness or ly to the word in the box. Print the new word on the line.

1. Gert stacked the cans ___neatly___ in rows.	neat
2. June played a tune ___softly___ on the organ.	soft
3. Ted felt helpless in the ___darkness___	dark
4. Betty chose her teammates ___wisely___	wise
5. The fire truck turned the corner ___quickly___	quick
6. Luke ___gladly___ helped his mother sweep.	glad
7. Our teacher likes ___neatness___ at all times.	neat
8. We were ___nearly___ at camp when it rained.	near
9. His ___sadness___ showed in his face.	sad

Lesson 45
Suffixes *ER* and *EST*   (pages 116–118)

Objective   The child will add the suffixes *er* and *est* to base words and identify the newly formed words in isolation and within sentences.

Review

Speaking/Reading   To practice recognition of base words and suffixes, flash the following word cards: *careful, harmless, playful, useless, dryness, sadness, safely, lately.* For each, have a child read the word and identify its base word and suffix.

Teaching Ideas

Listening   To introduce the concept of comparatives and superlatives, draw three items of increasing size on the chalkboard and use them in a simple story. As you speak, write the word *large, larger,* or *largest* under each appropriate drawing. Then, invite a volunteer to read each word and identify its base word and suffix. For example, draw three houses and tell the following story.

Once there were three brothers who each had a house. The first brother had a large house. The second brother had a house that was larger. But the third brother lived in the largest house of all.

To continue the lesson, ask a child to point to the big house of the first brother; have another child find a house that is bigger than the first one; and ask a third child to find the house that is the biggest of all. Explain that when two things are compared, we use the suffix *er,* but when three or more things are compared, we use the suffix *est.*

Speaking   Write the following sets of words on the chalkboard.

neat/neater/neatest	*hot/hotter/hottest*
small/smaller/smallest	*quick/quicker/quickest*
near/nearer/nearest	*tiny/tinier/tiniest*

For each set, invite a volunteer to read the three words and to circle the suffixes in the last two words. Challenge the child to use the set of words in a series of comparisons. An appropriate example of this might be the following.

I keep my room neat. My big brother keeps his room neater than I do. My mother keeps her room neatest of all.

Encourage the children to remember to use *er* to compare two items and *est* to compare three or more. Consider offering children who have difficulty thinking of comparisons a prompt such as: *Use hot, hotter, and hottest to compare the temperature in June, July, and August.*

Story Game   Write the following sets of words on the chalkboard: *dark/darker/darkest, fast/faster/fastest, thin/thinner/thinnest, late/later/latest.* For each set, invite a volunteer to begin a short story similar to the one you told about the houses in the Listening activity, using the first word in the set.

---

116   **Suffixes: ER, EST**

The letters er and est are suffixes. First review the rules for adding suffixes to base words. Then add er and est to each of the following words. Print the new words on the lines.

slow	slower	slowest
near	nearer	nearest
quick	quicker	quickest
hot	hotter	hottest
sad	sadder	saddest
thin	thinner	thinnest
late	later	latest
brave	braver	bravest
large	larger	largest
happy	happier	happiest
shiny	shinier	shiniest

Suffixes: ER, EST   **117**

Read the words that are part of each sentence. Finish the sentence by adding er or est to the word in the box. Print the new word on the line.

1. A jet flies _____ faster _____ than the fastest bird.	fast
2. That is the _____ biggest _____ city near here.	big
3. My pad of paper is _____ thicker _____ than yours.	thick
4. Why is this lamp _____ dimmer _____ than that one?	dim
5. Dessert will be served _____ later _____ .	late
6. Here is the _____ shadiest _____ spot on the beach.	shady
7. José has the _____ neatest _____ desk of all.	neat
8. This is the _____ widest _____ part of the river.	wide
9. The peacock is the _____ prettiest _____ bird of all.	pretty
10. It is _____ hotter _____ in summer than winter.	hot
11. Friday was the _____ sunniest _____ day of the week.	sunny

(For example: *One night there was a dark cloud over the moon. You couldn't see across the street.*) Let the child pick a classmate to continue the story using the word with the *er* suffix. (For example: *The next night the cloud was even darker. You couldn't see across the sidewalk.*) Then have this child select a third who is to finish the story using the word with the *est* suffix. (For example: *The third night the cloud was darkest of all. You couldn't even see your hand in front of your face.*)

Extension

Writing   Challenge the children to write and illustrate a story modeled after those told in the Story Game in the previous activity.

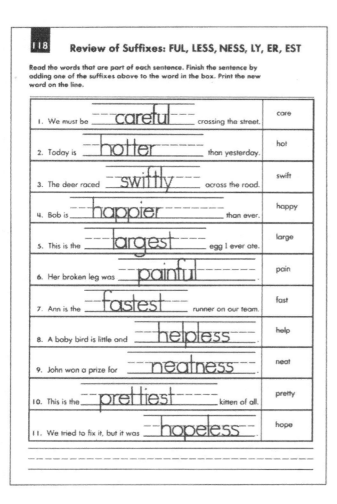

118   Review of Suffixes: FUL, LESS, NESS, LY, ER, EST

Read the words that are part of each sentence. Finish the sentence by adding one of the suffixes above to the word in the box. Print the new word on the line.

1.	We must be __careful__ crossing the street.	careful	care
2.	Today is __hotter__ than yesterday.	hotter	hot
3.	The deer raced __swiftly__ across the road.	swiftly	swift
4.	Bob is __happier__ than ever.	happier	happy
5.	This is the __largest__ egg I ever ate.	largest	large
6.	Her broken leg was __painful__.	painful	pain
7.	Ann is the __fastest__ runner on our team.	fastest	fast
8.	A baby bird is little and __helpless__.	helpless	help
9.	John won a prize for __neatness__.	neatness	neat
10.	This is the __prettiest__ kitten of all.	prettiest	pretty
11.	We tried to fix it, but it was __hopeless__.	hopeless	hope

Lesson 46
Contractions with *WILL* (page 119)

Objective The child will read and identify contractions in which *will* is shortened.

Review

Writing To review adding suffixes to base words, you may wish to write the following words on the chalkboard and invite the children to add the suffixes *s* or *es*, *ed*, and *ing* to each: *study, hurry, empty, try.* Write each appropriate suggestion on the chalkboard.

Teaching Ideas

Observing Display an air-filled balloon at the front of the classroom. Suggest that the children note the size of the balloon. Begin releasing air from the balloon and invite the children to describe what is happening to the balloon. The children will report that the balloon is getting smaller. To reinforce the children's responses, state that the balloon is *contracting*, or getting smaller. Explain that some words can be contracted, or made smaller, too.

Reading You might wish to write the following phrases on the chalkboard and ask the children to read each phrase aloud: *I will, she will, you will, we will, he will, they will.*

Explain to the children that you are going to contract these phrases, and erase the *wi* in each phrase. Insert an apostrophe in each erased space. (You may wish to rewrite the remaining letters and the apostrophe to eliminate extra letter space.) Then pronounce the contractions, and encourage the children to say the new words aloud. Point out to the children that each resulting word is called a *contraction*. Explain that a contraction is a short way of speaking or writing two words, and the mark between word parts is called an *apostrophe*. Point to the apostrophes on the chalkboard. Encourage the children to repeat the word *apostrophe* after you.

Extension

Writing Write the following sentences on the chalkboard.
1. *I'll go to the store for Mother.*
2. *She'll play with us.*
3. *He'll have one hundred pennies in his bank.*
4. *They'll have fun riding the ponies.*

Invite the child to read each sentence and circle the contraction on the chalkboard. To extend the activity further, encourage the child to write the phrase that forms the contraction.

78

Lesson 47
Contractions with *NOT* (page 120)

Objective The child will read and identify contractions in which *not* is shortened.

Review

Speaking To review forming contractions, you might write the following phrases on the chalkboard, underlining phrases as shown.

1. Ted says <u>he will</u> help.   *3. <u>She will</u> go home now.*
2. <u>I will</u> call my sister.   *4. <u>You will</u> like this snack.*

Invite volunteers to read a sentence aloud and name the contraction of the underlined phrase. Encourage the children to explain in their own words what contractions are and how they are formed.

Teaching Ideas

Writing You may wish to write the following phrases on the chalkboard: *is not, has not, do not, did not, have not, are not.* Erase the *O* in *is not* and invite a volunteer to form a contraction by writing an apostrophe in its place. (You may wish to rewrite the remaining letters and the apostrophe to eliminate extra letter space.) Pronounce the contraction and encourage the children to repeat it. Then invite the children to come forward and form other contractions by erasing the *O*s in the other phrases on the chalkboard and inserting apostrophes.

Extension

Writing Write the following phrases in a column on the chalkboard: *has not, is not, did not, have not, do not, are not.* Direct the child to copy the phrases on a sheet of paper. Encourage the child to write the appropriate contraction following each phrase.

Family Involvement Activity Duplicate the Family Letter on page 107 of this Teacher's Edition. Send it home with the children.

79

Lesson 48
Contractions with *IS* and *ARE* (page 121)

Objective   The child will read and identify contractions in which *are* and *is* are shortened.

Review

Speaking   To review the formation of contractions, you may wish to display the following phrases on cards at the front of the classroom: *he will, I will, she will, they will, are not, do not, have not, is not.* Invite volunteers to read a phrase aloud, state the appropriate contraction, and use the contraction in a sentence. To extend the review, you might challenge the children to spell the contractions aloud.

Teaching Ideas

Speaking   Write the following phrases in two columns on the chalkboard and ask volunteers to say each phrase: *he is, she is, it is; you are, we are, they are.* Tell the children that you will shorten the phrases in the first column by writing each as a contraction. Erase the letter *I* in *he is* and replace it with an apostrophe. Invite the children to read the resulting contraction and then to spell it aloud. Repeat the procedure for *she is* and *it is.* Continue the activity with the second column of words by erasing the *A* in each phrase and replacing it with an apostrophe.

Writing   To reinforce the lesson, you may wish to display the following phrases on cards at the front of the classroom: *he is, it is, they are, she is, we are, you are.* (You may provide these cards or have the children make them as part of the activity.) Invite volunteers, in turn, to choose a card and read the phrase on the card to the other children. Ask them to say the contraction that can be made from the phrase, and write it on the chalkboard. Encourage the children to write sentences using the contractions and to read the sentences aloud. Acknowledge correct responses.

Extension

Writing   Write on the chalkboard the following contractions: *he's, she'll, they're, it's, isn't, we're, I'll, you're.* Invite the child to write each contraction in a sentence. You may also wish to suggest that the child try creating a sentence using two of the contractions.

Contractions with Is and Are   121

Draw a line from the two words in the first column in each box to the one word in the second column that has the same meaning.

1.
he is — it's
she is — he's
it is — she's

2.
we are — you're
you are — we're
they are — they're

Print the contraction for each pair of words on the line.

1. you are   **you're**   2. she is   **she's**
3. he is   **he's**   4. they are   **they're**
5. we are   **we're**   6. it is   **it's**

Read each sentence below. Underline the contractions. Choose the correct meaning for each contraction from the list just above. Print the meaning on the line next to the sentence.

1. Most of us think it's too cold to skate.   **it is**
2. You're the one we're trying to cheer up.   **You are/we are**
3. They're the ones who made a fuss.   **They are**
4. He's crying, but she's not.   **He is / she is**

Lesson 49
Contractions with *AM*, *HAVE*, and *US* (pages 122–123)

Objective The child will read and identify contractions in which *am*, *have*, and *us* are shortened.

Teaching Ideas

Speaking You may wish to write the following phrases in two columns on the chalkboard: *I have, you have, we have, they have; let us, I am.* After encouraging the children to read each phrase in the first column aloud, lead the children in changing each phrase into a contraction. Erase the letters *HA* from the phrases in the first column. Invite volunteers to come forward and insert apostrophes in the blank spaces to complete the contractions. Encourage the children to pronounce the resulting contractions. Repeat the procedure with the phrases in the second column, erasing the *U* in *us* and the *A* in *am*.

Writing Present the following word cards to the children, one at a time: *I'm, I've, let's, they've, we've, you've.* Encourage the children to read each word card aloud, state the phrase from which the contraction is derived, and write the complete phrase on the chalkboard.

Home-Run Game You might wish to play the Home-Run Game as described in Lesson 37 in this unit, using cards that include the following phrases: *I will, did not, has not, is not, it is, we are, I am, we have.* Invite the children to read the phrases and to identify the appropriate contractions. With each correct response, allow the children to progress to the appropriate bases.

Reteaching

Reading You may wish to write the following phrases and contractions in two columns on the chalkboard: *I am, you will, are not, we have, they have, let us; aren't, you'll, I'm, we've, let's, they've.* Encourage the child to join you in reading aloud the phrases and words. Point out that each phrase in the first column corresponds with a contraction in the second column. Challenge the child to draw lines connecting the phrases to their corresponding contractions.

Extension

Writing Duplicate the following sentences on a sheet of paper.

1. *I have* a bag of nuts.
2. *Let us* help Dad.
3. *You have* been sad lately.
4. *He will* be a good player.
5. I *did not* tell her.
6. *I am* never late.

Direct the child to read the sentences and to write contractions after each sentence for the underlined phrases.

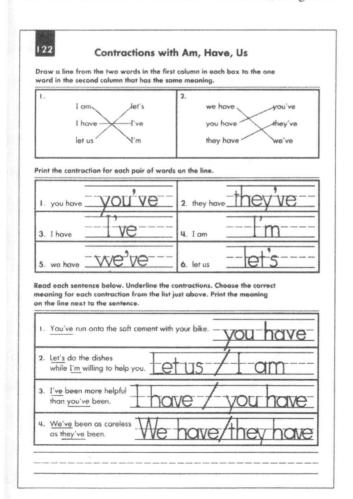

Lesson 50
Vowel Digraph *OO*　(pages 124–127)

Objective　The child will read and identify the two sounds of the vowel digraph *oo*.

A vowel digraph is a double vowel that does not follow Long Vowel Rule 1.

Review

Reading　To review the short and long vowel rules, you may wish to display the following word cards to the children: *crib, free, plane, slip, coat, with, branch, pony, we*. Encourage volunteers to read each word aloud and to name the vowel rule that applies to the word.

Teaching Ideas

Listening　Display a picture flashcard for the word *broom* or display a broom at the front of the classroom. Invite the children to name the picture or object, and to identify the vowel sound. Explain to the children that *oo* is called a *vowel digraph* (you may want to use the term *irregular double vowel*), and that it does not follow Long Vowel Rule 1. To

reinforce letter/sound association, you might want to write the word *broom* on the chalkboard and circle the *oo*.

Display pictures or picture flashcards for each of the following words: *school, rooster, moon, pool*. Invite volunteers to identify each picture and to repeat the *oo* vowel sound in each word.

To introduce the second pronunciation of the *oo* digraph, you might hold a book up in the front of the classroom and ask the children to identify it. Then, write the word *book* on the chalkboard and circle the *oo*. Encourage the children to repeat the vowel sound in the word *book*. Explain that the vowel sound in *book* is another sound of the vowel digraph *oo*. Guide children to discuss how the *oo* sound in *broom* is different from the *oo* sound in *book*.

Speaking　You might want to develop the children's understanding of the *oo* digraph through a series of rhyming words. Write the key words *noon* and *look* on the chalkboard. Say the word *noon* aloud and encourage the children to suggest other words that rhyme with *noon* and that have the digraph *oo*. The children might suggest words such as the following: *moon, spoon, loon, soon*. Write the children's suggestions on the chalkboard and challenge them to use each word in a sentence. Repeat the activity using the key word *look*. The children might suggest words such as the following: *book, cook, nook, hook, rook*.

Print the following pairs of words on the chalkboard: *moan/moon, brook/broke, food/fond, stood/steed*. Invite volunteers to each read a word pair aloud and to circle the word that contains the digraph. Encourage the children to explain how words with digraphs are different from words that follow Long Vowel Rule 1.

Writing Stack the following word cards facedown on a desk at the front of the classroom: *choose, book, food, goose, stood, took, soon, fool, room, bloom.* Encourage the children to choose a word card from the stack, read it aloud, come forward, and then write a sentence using the word on the chalkboard.

Extension

Art You might encourage the child to create a picture book for a riddle that uses the *oo* digraph. Direct the child to fold a large sheet of paper in half. Suggest that the child write the *oo* digraph on the front page. On the inside, have the child draw a picture clue for an *oo* word. On the opposite page, encourage the child to draw a blank for each letter of the word that the picture clue represents. You might suggest that the child fill in the digraph *oo*. Direct the child to write the word for the object on the back page. Encourage the child to share the picture book with others, asking them to guess the correct word for the picture. If the child has time to complete several picture riddles, you might want to help the child staple them together into a large book. Acknowledge the creativity or design of the drawings.

Digraph Dictionary As a further extension, encourage the child to look through newspapers and magazines for words with the digraph *oo*. Direct the child to copy the words on a sheet of paper. You might help the child organize these words in alphabetical order. Ask the child to define the familiar words by drawing a picture for each or writing a sentence that tells what each word means. Encourage the child to save this "dictionary" page for reference. You might want to suggest that the child add to this digraph dictionary in future lessons.

---

126   **Vowel Digraph Sound: OO**

The word book has the other sound of the vowel digraph oo. Say the name of the picture in each box. Circle each picture with a name that has the sound of oo, as in book.

1. book	2. feet	3. hood	4. bird
5. foot	6. woods	7. block	8. hook
9. toad	10. fork	11. cook	12. cookies
13. brook	14. woodpecker	15. sled	16. bread
17. goat	18. wheat	19. woodpile	20. football

Say the name of the picture in each box. Circle its name.

1.	foot / food / boot	2.	books / boots / foot	3.	roots / woods / wools
4.	mood / noon / moon	5.	hood / hoof / foot	6.	soon / zoo / moo
7.	root / cook / took	8.	tooth / fools / tools	9.	hook / look / book
10.	footprint / footpath / football	11.	look / hook / book	12.	book / hook / brook
13.	cooler / coops / cookies	14.	woodshed / woodsman / woodpile	15.	woodcutter / woodpecker / woodcraft

---

Vowel Digraph Sound: OO   **127**

Read the words that are part of each sentence. Circle the word in the box that will finish the sentence. Print the word on the line.

1. Look at the horses run.	Book / Look / Hook
2. One of them has hurt its foot .	tool / boot / foot
3. They are shearing wool from the sheep.	wool / cool / food
4. Janet took the thick book to school.	took / book / brook
5. Who can give me a good haircut?	good / pool / food
6. Please give me a book for my birthday.	took / book / look
7. May I please have some wood carving tools, too?	wool / wood / hood
8. They took turns swinging and riding the bike.	took / look / book
9. Who will put the worm on the hook for me?	look / book / hook
10. Dora had a jacket with a hood on it.	food / hood / hoop
11. We'll camp in the woods and cook our meals there.	cool / wool / cook

---

Lesson 51
Vowel Digraph *EA*   (pages 128–129)

Objective   The child will associate the vowel digraph *ea* with its sound.

Review

Speaking   To review the *ea* combination in words that contain the long vowel sound, you may wish to write the following words on the chalkboard: *speak, clean, seal, meat.* Invite volunteers to read the words aloud, identify the vowel sound, and explain Long Vowel Rule 1.

Teaching Ideas

Listening   Explain to the children that *ea* can also represent another vowel sound. Present a picture flashcard for the word *bread* and write the word *bread* on the chalkboard. Encourage the children to say the word and to listen for the vowel sound. Explain to them that *ea* is a vowel digraph (you may want to use the term *irregular double vowel*) and that it does not follow Long Vowel Rule 1. Encourage the children to identify the name of the *ea* sound in *bread.*

Speaking   Write the following words in two columns on the chalkboard: *bread, head, thread; leather, weather, feather.* Pronounce each word for the children, encouraging them to repeat the words after you. You may also invite the children to use the words in short rhymes. For example, you might choose the words *bread* and *head* for the following rhyme: *He shook his head/ when he saw the bread.*

Writing   Write the following word pairs on the chalkboard: *head/bead, bread/breed, sweat/sweet, thread/read.* Invite volunteers to come forward and to circle the word in each pair that contains the *ea* digraph. Then suggest they write a sentence using the word.

Extension

Writing   Write the following sentences on the chalkboard.

1. *Danny bumped his head in the darkness.*
2. *I read that book last year.*
3. *Lee spread peanut butter on her bread.*
4. *Dad used red thread to mend his socks.*

Challenge the child to circle the words in each sentence that have the *ea* digraph. Encourage the child to copy the words in alphabetical order on a separate sheet of paper. If you wish, you may encourage the child to create a digraph dictionary page using these words. (The child may add this page to the digraph dictionary if the Extension activity in the previous lesson was done.)

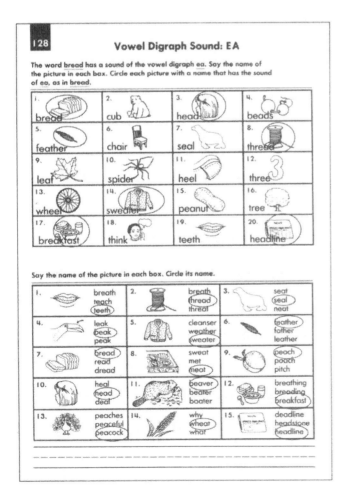

Lesson 52
Vowel Digraphs *AU* and *AW*   (pages 130–131)

Objective   The child will identify the sounds of the vowel digraphs *au* and *aw* appearing in isolation and in words.

Review

To practice recognition of the vowel digraphs *oo* and *ea*, you may wish to write the following words on the chalkboard: *feather, hook, spoon, look, head, too, zoo, good, bread*. Invite volunteers to read a word, underline the vowel digraph, and use the word in a sentence.

Teaching Ideas

Listening   You might display a model car and a straw at the front of the classroom. Write the words *auto* and *straw* on the chalkboard. Invite the children to listen for the vowel sound in each word as you say it. Point out that *au* and *aw* have the same sound. Explain to the children that *au* and *aw* are *vowel digraphs* (you may want to use the term *irregular double vowels*) and that they do not follow Long Vowel Rule 1.

Speaking   You might wish to display the following word cards: *crawl, draw, Paul, because, saw, pause, claw*. En-

by s
at the
following
feather, saw
teer from one
the word silently,
help the team gues
maximum number of a
the team guesses the wor
the word, allow the other t
word. Continue the game unti
used. The team with the most poi

Extension

Writing   Write the following senten
board, and ask the child to come forward a
words containing *au* or *aw* digraphs.
1. *The farmer hauled bales of straw.*
2. *The hawk catches food with its claws.*
3. *Paul used the hacksaw to cut wood.*
4. *The awning shades the auto and the lawn.*
Encourage the child to select a circled word and to create another sentence using the word. Acknowledge correct word usage in a sentence.

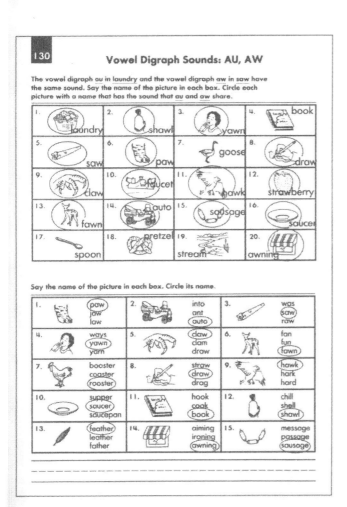

Write the following key words in a row on the
ʔok, saw, bread, food, auto. Encourage the
e forward and to underline the digraph in each
gest that the children list under each key word
h the same digraph.

You might write the following sentences on

ʔawn in the woods.
ʔers stood in the woodpile.
ʔeather will get cooler.
ʔl clever Paul?

ead the sentences and to circle the words
. If you wish, you may encourage the child
ʔe words to the digraph dictionary.

ʔement Activity   Duplicate the Family
ʔf this Teacher's Edition. Send it home

---

courage the children to read each word and identify its vowel
digraph.

Picture-Clue-Team Game   Challenge the children
ʔacking word cards for vowel digraphs facedown on a desk
ʔront of the classroom. You might include cards for the
words: *book, paw, rooster, sausage, moon, bread.*
Divide the class into two teams. Invite a volun-
ʔam to choose a word card from the stack, read
and draw picture clues on the chalkboard to
ʔe the word. Establish a time limit or a
ʔtempts in which to guess the word. If
ʔassign a point. If they do not guess the
ʔam an opportunity to guess the
ʔall the word cards have been
ʔts wins the game.

ʔces on the chalk-
ʔd to circle the

ʔard. Continue the activity

Review of Vowel Digraphs

Read the words that are part of each sentence. Circle the word in the box
that will finish the sentence. Print the word on the line.

1.	The weather is hot in **August**	March / (August) / May
2.	Camping is good **because** of the weather.	between / saucer / (because)
3.	Please turn off the leaky **faucet**	(faucet) / fancy / furnace
4.	Fido must not eat **raw** meat.	saw / was / (raw)
5.	Grace toasted the **bread**	lead / (bread) / tread
6.	Let's **choose** a good birthday gift for Ken.	shoot / chose / (choose)
7.	Jane **took** a book back to the library.	book / (took) / look
8.	The **fawn** darted into the woods.	fan / (fawn) / farm
9.	The class **saw** the workers make steel.	(saw) / was / sad
10.	A stalled car **caused** a traffic jam.	hauled / paused / (caused)
11.	Tom handed his uncle the **saw**	raw / law / (saw)

Unit 10 Diphthongs

Diphthongs *OW* and *OU*   (pages 133–136)

Objective   The child will identify *ow* and *ou* diphthongs appearing in isolation and in words.

A diphthong consists of two vowels blended together to form one sound.

Review

Speaking   To practice quick recognition of words containing *W* as a vowel, you may wish to display the following word cards: *blow, bow, mow, show, snow*. Invite the children to read the words aloud, identify the long *O* sound, and use the words in sentences. Encourage the children to explain how Long Vowel Rule 1 applies to these words.

Teaching Ideas

Listening   You may wish to present pictures or picture flashcards for *clown* and *house*. Say the name of each picture, then write the word on the chalkboard. Encourage the children to repeat the words, listening for the vowel sound in each. As the children say the words, underline the *ow* in clown and the *ou* in house. Point out to the children that the *ow* and *ou* have the same sound. Explain that the *ow* and *ou* in these words are called diphthongs because they are blended together to create one vowel sound.

Writing   Display the following word cards on the chalkboard ledge and read the words aloud: *house, loud, cow, town, down, flowers*. Then duplicate the following sentences on paper or write them on the chalkboard.

   1. The mouse lives in the old _____ .
   2. The crowd at the game was very _____ .
   3. The sow and the owl live on the farm with the _____ .
   4. She put on a long gown to go to _____ .
   5. It was funny to see the clown fall _____ .
   6. April showers bring May _____ .

Invite the children to read each sentence aloud. Challenge them to fill in each blank by using a word from the word cards. Have a volunteer write the correct words in the blanks or on the chalkboard. When each word has been written, encourage the children to circle the words in each sentence that contain an *ow* or *ou* diphthong. If you wish, you may ask a volunteer to read aloud all the words that contain diphthongs.

Speaking   Display the following word cards and ask the children to read the words and to use them in sentences: *cow, owl, scout, towel, cloud, blouse, snout.*

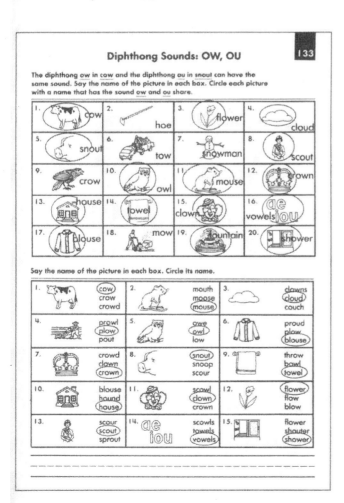

Now write the following columns of words on the chalkboard.

tow	*growl*	*shower*	*flour*	*cloud*
show	*throw*	*rainbow*	*fellow*	*grown*
cow	*flow*	*slow*	*flower*	*clown*

Invite volunteers to each read a column of words and to identify the diphthongs. Ask each volunteer to circle the diphthong in each word and to use the words in sentences.

Picture-Clue-and-Riddle Game   Challenge the children with this game. Stack the following word cards facedown on a desk at the front of the classroom: *sour, towel, proud, brown, growl, hour, vowel, found, down, hound.* Encourage volunteers, in turn, to choose a word card from the stack, read it silently, and draw a picture clue for the word on the chalkboard. Let each volunteer invite other children to guess the word. If the children have trouble guessing the word, suggest that the volunteer add a sentence clue. (For example, for the word *sour*, a volunteer might draw a lemon. For a sentence clue, the child might write, *When something is not sweet, it is* _____ .) Invite the child who guesses correctly to choose the next word card from the stack and to provide the clues.

Reteaching

Reading   Write the following sentences on the chalkboard.

1. *The silly clown had a brown mouse.*
2. *Let's count the cows and crows.*
3. *How did the scouts grow such big flowers?*
4. *The cowboy shouted to the crowd.*

Encourage the child to read each sentence aloud with you and to underline the vowels. Suggest that the child look at the underlined letters and circle the vowels that form diphthongs. Point out that *ow* forms a long vowel sound in some words and a diphthong in others.

Extension

Writing   You might give the child a sheet of blank newsprint folded in half and crayons or markers. Encourage the child to write a sentence containing a diphthong on one half of the paper and to illustrate the sentence on the other half.

Lesson 55
Diphthongs *OY* and *OI* (pages 137–138)

Objective   The child will associate *oy* and *oi* with their respective sounds.

Review

Writing   To review adding suffixes to base words, you may wish to write the following words on the chalkboard and ask the children to add the suffixes *er* and *est* to them: *slow, proud, brown, round, loud, safe, hot, pretty.* Encourage the children to use each new word in a sentence.

To extend the activity and review *ou* and *ow* diphthongs, you might invite volunteers to name the words with *ou* and *ow* diphthongs and to suggest other words that contain these diphthongs.

Teaching Ideas

Listening   Display pictures or picture flashcards of a boy and of a pile of coins. Say the name of each picture and print it on the chalkboard, encouraging the children to listen for the vowel sound in each word. Underline the *oy* and *oi* and invite the children to repeat the sound the letters make. Point out that *oy* and *oi* have the same sound in these words. Explain to the children that *oy* and *oi* are called diphthongs because they create a new vowel sound when they are blended to-

gether. Challenge the children to name other words that contain the sound made by the *oy* and *oi* diphthongs. The children might name words such as the following: *noise, toy, joy, soil.*

Writing   Display the following picture flashcards on the chalkboard ledge: *boy, coin, oil, soil, toy, coil, point.* Tell the children that each picture represents a word that has an *oy* or *oi* diphthong. Challenge the children to identify each picture and to write on the chalkboard the word for the object in the picture. You may need to guide the children in spelling the words correctly. Encourage volunteers to create sentences using the words written on the chalkboard.

Extension

Art   Ask the child to look through magazines for words containing *oy* and *oi* diphthongs. You might want to encourage the child to search also for words containing *ow* and *ou* diphthongs. Suggest that the child cut out the words and paste them onto a sheet of paper to create a diphthong collage.

Lesson 56
Diphthong *EW* (pages 139–140)

Objective   The child will identify the sound of the diphthong *ew* in isolation and within words.

Review

Name-the-*Oy* Game   Take time to review the *oi* and *oy* diphthongs. Write the following sentences on the chalkboard, underlining the incomplete word in each.

1. *Some children are girls and some are __ oys. (boys)*
2. *When the water in the tea kettle gets hot, it begins to __ oi __ . (boil)*
3. *When you are very happy, you are full of __ oy. (joy)*
4. *On the telephone, someone can hear the sound of your __ oi ___ . (voice)*
5. *Children like to play with __ oys. (toys)*

Ask volunteers to complete the word containing the *oy* or *oi* sound that answers each clue. To extend the activity, invite the children to think of other *oy* and *oi* words and to make up clues for them.

Teaching Ideas

Listening   To introduce the diphthong *ew*, print the following words on the chalkboard: *blew, grew, few, new*. Have the children listen for the *ew* vowel sound as they repeat each word after you. Underline the *ew* sound in each word, and ask for its vowel sound. Then tell the children that *e* and *w* work together to make a single vowel sound. This is the sound they can hear in *grew* and *few*. You may want to remind the children that they already have learned other diphthongs including *oi, oy, ou,* and *ow*.

Reading   Write the following sentences on tagboard strips or on the chalkboard.

1. *Dad used his screwdriver on the screw.*
2. *Roy drew with his new pencil.*
3. *Roni served beef stew to a few friends.*
4. *That boy threw his chewing gum away.*

For each sentence, call on a volunteer to read the sentence aloud and then name the words with the *ew* diphthong. (You may wish to keep these sentences on the chalkboard for the Extension activity.)

Extension

Writing   Point out that each of the sentences used in the Reading activity have more than one word with the *ew* diphthong. Challenge the child to create a sentence that has as many *ew* diphthongs as possible. If the child uses words such as *through, too,* and *you*, point out the similarity of the vowel sounds. Write the incorrect words on the chalkboard to provide a visual confirmation that the choices are incorrect for *ew* diphthongs. You may want to have the child write out the sentence and circle the *ew* words.

139

Diphthong Sound: EW

The word blew has the sound of the diphthong ew. Say the name of the picture in each box. Circle each picture with a name that has the sound of ew.

| 1. blew | 2. screw | 3. jewelry | 4. sewer |
| 5. bowl | 6. screwdriver | 7. snowman | 8. newspaper |

Read each question. Choose the answer from the list below. Print the answer on the line in the box.

chew   mew   stew   flew   few   news   blew

1. What must you do to your food before you swallow it?	chew
2. What did the wind do to the kite?	blew
3. How did the birds travel to the south?	flew
4. What is the sound made by a cat?	mew
5. If you didn't have many coins, how many would you have?	few
6. What may be good or bad? You hear about it in many ways.	news
7. What can you eat?	stew

140

Diphthong Sound: EW

Read the words that are part of each sentence. Circle the word in the box that will finish the sentence. Print the word on the line.

1. Jack ____ grew ____ tall.	blew / (grew) / dew
2. Who ____ threw ____ this chewing gum on the floor?	screw / stew / (threw)
3. Where did you get that shiny ____ new ____ coin?	(new) / now / mew
4. The wind ____ blew ____ hard, but the house didn't fall.	(few) / blew / blow
5. We joined two blocks of wood with a ____ screw ____ .	threw / new / (screw)
6. Tom's uncle ____ drew ____ cartoons for the class.	chew / grow / (drew)
7. The ____ dew ____ in the morning sun looked like jewels.	do / (dew) / few
8. Did you hear the cat ____ mew ____ ?	pew / grew / (mew)
9. Just a ____ few ____ children can make a lot of noise.	dew / (few) / flew
10. Manny wore his ____ new ____ winter coat.	grew / (new) / drew
11. The ____ crew ____ got on the ship.	chew / (crew) / brew

90

Lesson 57
Review of Diphthongs (pages 141–142)

Objective   The child will associate the diphthongs *ou*, *ow*, *oi*, *oy*, and *ew* with their respective sounds in words appearing in context.

Review

Picture-Clue Game   To provide additional practice in recognizing vowel digraph sounds, prepare word cards for the following words: *book, cookies, football, thread, bread, moon, broom, spoon.* Ask a volunteer to come forward, choose one of the cards, and then draw picture clues on the chalkboard. Explain that the artist must not verbalize any clues. You may wish to offer the child who correctly guesses the word a chance to draw the next picture. Pictures might be labeled by a volunteer when the correct response is given.

Teaching Ideas

Diphthong Relay Race   Consider a relay race format to give children practice in using words with the diphthongs *oy, oi, ow, ou,* and *ew*. Write out the following column headings and incomplete words on the chalkboard.

OY or EW	OI or OU	OY or OW	OW or EW
b __ __	c __ __ n	j __ __	cl __ __ n
st __ __	sh __ __ t	n __ __	t __ __ n
f __ __	r __ __ nd	h __ __	scr __ __
t __ __	j __ __ n	d __ __ n	d __ __
bl __ __	p __ __ nt	enj __ __	__ __ l

Assign one column to each of four teams. Have the first child on each team come forward, correctly complete the word with one of the two diphthongs at the top of the column, and then sit down before the second child on the team can go to the chalkboard to complete the next word.

Before beginning, you may use one or two items as samples to help the children understand that there will be only one correct answer for each incomplete word.

Extension

Writing Rhymes   Challenge a child to write a short rhyming poem of three or four lines, using diphthong words. You may want to provide the following word bank of appropriate rhyming words that have the targeted diphthongs.

1. *found/round/sound/pound/mound*
2. *noise/boys/joys/toys*
3. *now/cow/how/plow*
4. *few/grew/new/stew/screw/threw/drew*

141

Diphthongs

Read the words that are part of each rhyme. Choose the word from the box that will finish the rhyme. Print the word on the line.

1. A sly old mouse Came into the _____	house	home hound house
2. He ate some beef stew And had breadcrumbs, a _____	few	new few coil
3. The cat and the boy Were busy with a _____	toy	toy threw towel
4. The mouse never made a sound So he was never _____	found	found round frown
5. The cat felt blue, And so it cried, "_____"	mew	few mew wow

Read the words that are part of each sentence. Finish the sentence by writing the words from the box in the correct order.

1. The bike is _____	shiny and new	and new shiny
2. I will invite _____	all the boys	the all boys
3. The shop is on the main _____	street in town	town in street
4. Juan will dress _____	like a clown	a clown like
5. Did you buy a ticket _____?	with your coins	coins your with

---

142

Diphthongs

Read the short story. Then answer the questions at the bottom of the page.

Floyd's Birthday Surprise

On Floyd's seventh birthday he had a party. All the boys and girls from his class were invited.

Jim and Joy came first with a toy for Floyd. Soon the other boys and girls came. One gave a stuffed owl to Floyd. Another gave him a down puppet. Joyce gave him a gift of a tame white mouse.

The boys and girls sang, "Happy Birthday." They ate huge mounds of ice cream with cake.

Soon it was time for games. The boys and girls shouted as they threw coins into a bowl and pinned the tail on the donkey. Then they went outside to play tag around the swimming pool. Around and around they went, making more and more noise as they ran.

Suddenly, the noise stopped. There wasn't a sound. Dad looked out and saw the children pointing at the water. He knew what must have happened.

Quickly, he ran outside. "We didn't plan to scare you," he said. "This seal is our surprise gift to Floyd."

All of the boys and girls shouted with glee, and when they left the party, they agreed that they had never had so much fun.

1. What stuffed animal did Floyd get for a gift?	owl
2. What live animal did Joyce give Floyd?	mouse
3. In one game the children used a bowl and some coins. What did they do with the coins?	threw
4. What stopped when the boys and girls saw the seal in the pool?	noise

Lesson 58

KN (pages 143–144)

Objective The child will identify the sound of *kn* in isolation and within words.

Review

Reading To provide the children with additional practice in hearing the syllable break in compounds and other two-syllable words, write the following words on the chalkboard.

muffin	*bedspread*	*pencil*	*squirted*
sailboat	*dustpan*	*snowing*	*catfish*
hiking	*roundness*	*sawdust*	*downtown*

For each word, have a volunteer read the word aloud and then draw a diagonal line between the two syllables. Then have the child circle the whole word if it is a compound word.

Teaching Ideas

Listening You may wish to introduce the *kn* sound by knocking on the classroom door and then asking the children to identify your action. Print *knock* on the chalkboard, circle the *kn*, and say its sound. Explain that when *k* appears before *n* in a word, the *k* is silent while the *n* is heard.

Then-and-Now Game Children may enjoy learning that 500 years ago, people did pronounce the silent *k* in *kn* words. Explain that you are going to say some words as they might have been said 500 years ago. Challenge the children to identify the modern word. As an example, you might say: *500 years ago people would talk about "kuh-nights" in shining armor.* Proceed to use the following words in a sentence, being sure to pronounce the initial *k*: *doorknob, knee, knit, knife, kneel, knew.* For each, have a volunteer tell how we now pronounce the word. As each word is identified, write it on the chalkboard and ask the child who responded correctly to circle the *kn*.

Extension

Speaking The child may not be familiar with the *kn* words *knickknack* and *knapsack.* Consider writing these words on the chalkboard and then stating a defining sentence for each, for example: *Some people collect little statues or trinkets called knickknacks.* Challenge the child to read each of the words and to create a sentence for each.

Reading Write the following sentences on the chalkboard or duplicate them on a sheet of paper.

1. *Do you know how to knit?*
2. *Use a knife to cut the knot.*
3. *The dog knew how to turn the doorknob.*
4. *Pepe scraped his knuckles and his knees.*

For each, ask a child to read the sentence and then circle the words that use the *kn* sound.

Lesson 59

WR (pages 145–146)

Objective The child will associate *wr* with its sound.

Teaching Ideas

Listening Point to your wrist, asking the children to name that part of the arm. When a child responds correctly, write the word *wrist* on the chalkboard. Then point to a ring, asking the children to name it. When a child responds correctly, write *ring* on the chalkboard. Have the children listen for the beginning sound in *wrist* and in *ring* as they repeat each word after you. Ask if the two beginning sounds are the same or different. Explain to the children that when *w* appears before *r* in a word, the *w* is silent while the *r* is heard. You may want to point out that the rule for *wr* is similar to the rule for *kn*.

Reading/Listening Write the following phrases on the chalkboard.

1. *read the wrapper*
2. *around my wrist*
3. *wrote a riddle*
4. *wrecked my radio*
5. *a typewritten report*

For each, invite a volunteer to read the phrase and identify the two words that have the *r* sound. Then have the child circle the word with *wr*.

For further practice, write the following words and incomplete sentences on the chalkboard.

wrong   wrist   write   wreck
1. *I'll _____ a letter to him today.*
2. *Marta hurt her _____ .*
3. *That car was in a bad _____ .*
4. *It is _____ to tell a lie.*

For each sentence, ask a volunteer to find the correct word and then to read the sentence aloud.

Speaking Some children may not be familiar with the following words: *wreath, wring, wren,* and *wrench.* Consider writing each word on the chalkboard and challenging a volunteer to read and then explain the meaning of each word. Encourage the children to think of an original sentence in which the targeted word is used correctly.

Extension

Art To build recognition of the *wr* and *kn* sounds, write the following words on the chalkboard: *knee, wreath, wrapper, wren, wrench, knot, wring, writer.* Invite the child to draw pictures illustrating the words on a sheet of paper. Have the child write the name of each illustration on the other side of the paper and circle the targeted silent consonants. Additionally, you might have the child draw a stick figure and label the parts of the body that have the *wr* or *kn* sound (*wrist, knuckle, knee*).

WR | 145

The letters wr have the sound of r. The w is silent. Say the name of the picture in each box. Circle its name.

1.	2.	3.
(write) white	wren wreath	wreck (wrap)
4.	5.	6.
(wring) wing	(wrench) ranch	whip (typewriter)

Read each riddle below. Choose the answer from the list of words. Print the answer on the line in the box.

wren   wrapper   wreck   wreath   wrist

1. I may be made of flowers and leaves. I form a big ring. What am I?	wreath
2. I am the paper around a candy bar. What am I?	wrapper
3. I am the part of your arm next to your hand. What am I?	wrist
4. If you are a careless driver, you will soon know me. What am I?	wreck
5. I am a small bird with a twitching tail and a nice song. What am I?	wren

---

146 | WR

Read the words that are part of each sentence. Write the numeral of the word that will finish the sentence.

1.	
I have a new bracelet on my __4__	1. write
The train never had a __3__	2. wrote
Do you know how to __1__ letters?	3. wreck
Elaine __2__ a letter to her pal, Jeff.	4. wrist

2.	
I need some red __2__ paper.	1. written
Ned __4__ a poem for the school paper.	2. wrapping
He has __1__ stories and books, too.	3. wren
Where does the __3__ have its nest?	4. wrote

3.	
Don __2__ a package to send to Joe.	1. wrist
Joan fell and broke her __1__	2. wrapped
Bill __4__ for tickets to the circus.	3. wring
Please __3__ the water out of the cloth.	4. wrote

4.	
We used a __4__ to fix the sink.	1. wrecker
Aunt Flora wore a __2__ of roses in her hair.	2. wreath
The __1__ pulled the car out of the ditch.	3. wrong
"It is __3__ to tell a lie," said Nate to Abe.	4. wrench

Lesson 60
Ending LE   (pages 147–148)

Objective   The child will read words with the *le* ending in isolation and in sentences.

Review

Writing   To practice discrimination of the vowel sounds followed by *R*, have the children circle the vowel plus *R* in each of the following words you write on the chalkboard: *car, girls, horse, ladder, tiger, zipper, slippers, star, shirt*. Have the children read each word aloud.

Teaching Ideas

Listening   To introduce the *le* sound, show the children a picture of an apple, asking them to identify it. When a child responds correctly, write the word on the chalkboard and have the children listen for the sound of the *le* ending as they repeat the word after you. Underline the *le* and explain that when a word ends in *le*, you hear the *l* sound and the *e* is silent.

Word-Clue Game   Consider using the following guessing game to provide more extensive practice in hearing the *le* sound. Write the following words on the chalkboard: *marble, riddle, kettle, handle, sprinkle, rattle, pickle, whistle, bubble, steeple, little, grumble, wiggle*.

Have the children read the words aloud with you. Then tell the children that you will provide a clue for one of the words and ask them to guess the word. Give a clue sentence such as, *I am thinking of a word that ends in* le *and means very small*. When a child responds correctly, you may want to have that child circle the *le* ending in the word. You can then invite the child to make up a clue for another word. To reinforce the targeted sound, encourage a child to start his or her clue with the phrase, *I am thinking of a word that ends in* le. . . .

Reading   Write the following sentences on the chalkboard.

1. *Pia had some marbles and a whistle.*
2. *Tani's turtle likes to nibble on a pickle.*
3. *Some people have a candle on the dinner table.*
4. *The baby had a purple rattle.*

Call on a child to read each sentence and circle the words with the *le* ending. To test comprehension, you might ask questions about content such as, *What does Tani's turtle like to eat?*

Extension

Writing   Consider challenging the child to use as many *le* words as possible in a single, understandable sentence. You may want to suggest that the child use the words already on the board as a word bank. Have the child write the sentence on a tagboard strip. Post the sentence on the bulletin board.

147

Word Ending: LE

Read the short story. Then answer the questions at the bottom of the page.

The Fun Fair

The children planned the school fun fair. Each class made a booth for playing games or for making crafts.

Merle is in the third grade. Her class made a game booth. They set up a table and covered it with a cloth. They filled a large plastic bottle with sudsy water. When people came to their booth, the children gave each person a bubble wand to dip in the bottle. The person who blew the biggest bubble was the winner of the game. The prize was a whistle.

Todd is in the fourth grade. His class had a craft booth. They set up a table and chairs. They put out paper and pans of paints. When people came to their booth, they made a print. Each person took a slice of cut up vegetable or apple. They dipped their slices into the paints and pressed them on their papers. They had to handle the slices carefully to make a clear print.

Mike's fifth-grade class made a booth for turtle races. They made a track with boards. Each little turtle had its own slot. When Mike blew a whistle the race began. The turtles began to waddle down the track. Mike had no trouble guessing which turtle would win the race.

Everyone had a good time. They all agreed to have a fun fair each year.

1. A prize was given for the biggest	bubble
2. The prize was a	whistle
3. An art print was made with a slice of cut-up vegetable or	apple
4. The race was won by the fastest	turtle

148

Word Ending: LE

Read each question. Choose the answer from the list of words. Print the answer on the line in the box.

bubbles	marbles	pineapple	uncle	table
teakettle	stable	needle	buckle	purple

1. What has one eye but can't see?	needle
2. What has four legs but no feet?	table
3. What can you use to play a game?	marbles
4. I'm filled with water and placed on the fire. When water bubbles, I whistle. What am I?	teakettle
5. They float like feathers and are full of air. What are they?	bubbles
6. What looks like a huge pine cone and is good to eat?	pineapple
7. What color do red and blue make?	purple
8. What is your father's or your mother's brother to you?	uncle
9. I am a home for horses. What is my name?	stable
10. What holds a belt together?	buckle

94

Unit 12 Prefixes

Lesson 61
Prefixes *RE, UN,* and *DIS* (pages 149–152)

Objective The child will form and read words beginning with the prefixes *re, un,* and *dis* in isolation and within sentences.

Teaching Ideas

Listening Write the following words on the chalk-board in rows: *read, fill, paint, clean, tie, wrap, obey, trust, like.* Use these words to introduce the prefixes *re, un,* and *dis.* Explain that new words can be formed by adding letters to the beginnings of words. As an example, point out that instead of telling the children to "write the word again" you could give the direction to "rewrite" the word. Print the word *rewrite* on the chalkboard and circle the *re.* Have the children repeat the word after you, identifying the sound of the prefix *re.*

Now refer the children to the first row of words on the chalkboard. For each, call on a child to come forward and rewrite the base word, adding the prefix *re.* Have the child read the new word and explain its meaning, for example: *The word reread means to read again.*

Let the children know that you will introduce two more prefixes that change the meaning of the base word in a similar way. Write the word pairs *fair/unfair* and *obey/disobey* on the chalkboard, and ask volunteers to explain the difference in meaning between the two words in each pair. Encourage the children to offer concrete examples. Circle the prefixes *un* and *dis.* Explain that the prefix *un* means "not" or "the opposite of" while *dis* means "not" or "do not." Invite a volunteer to add the prefix *un* to the three words in the second row and to explain the new meaning of each word. Have another child add the prefix *dis* to the three words in row three and explain each change in word meaning.

Find-Your-Partner Game To provide additional exercise in recognizing the targeted prefixes, play the Find-Your-Partner Game. Distribute word cards on which you have written words and phrases such as the following: *make again, not clean, not obedient, not pleased, not paid, not safe, not true, remake, fill again, unclean, disobedient, displeased, unpaid, unsafe, untrue, refill.* Explain that each child who has two words on the card is to find a partner who has the word card with one word that uses a prefix and a base word to say the same thing. Have partners show both cards to the class and read them aloud. Ask the child holding the card with the prefix to call on a classmate who will write the word on the chalkboard, drawing a line between the prefix and the base word. Let the child who is holding the two-word card pick someone else to use the new word in a sentence. (You may wish to save the word cards for the Extension activity.)

---

149 **Prefix: RE**

The word refill is re + fill. Re is a prefix, and fill is the base word. A prefix is a word part that is added to the beginning of a base word. Circle the prefix in each word below. Underline the base word.

reread | remake | repoint | rewrite
respell | reprint | reseal | rewax
renew | reclaim | recount | retell
refill | repay | renumber | repack

Read each sentence. Choose the one word from the list above that could be used to make the sentence shorter. Print that word on the line.

1. When I tell the story again, I will act it out.	retell
2. Take a slice of bread, but seal the wrapper again.	reseal
3. The gas tank is empty, so we will have to fill it again.	refill
4. After we repaint the walls, we will wax the floors again.	rewax
5. Write your name again until you can write it well.	rewrite
6. Ann, please read the sentence in a louder voice.	reread
7. The next time, we will make valentines on good paper.	remake
8. I counted the coins, but I will have to count them again.	recount

---

150 **Prefix: UN**

The word unwise is un + wise. Un is a prefix, and wise is the base word. Circle the prefix of each word below. Underline the base word.

untie | unwrap | untidy | unhappy
unlock | undress | unfair | unselfish
unpin | unload | unwilling | unsafe
unpack | unscrew | untrue | unable

Read the words that are part of each sentence. Then circle the word that will finish the sentence. Print the word on the line.

1. It is time to ___ and go to bed.	unpin / unlock / undress	undress
2. You must wait until your birthday to ___ the gifts.	unwrap / unscrew / unsafe	unwrap
3. Some people tell stories that are ___ .	untie / untrue / untidy	untrue
4. It is ___ to play too near the river.	unable / unsafe / unfair	unsafe
5. Mike was ___ and gave Kim some of his lunch.	unselfish / unfair / unwilling	unselfish
6. Bill cannot ___ the knot in the kite string.	unpin / unpack / untie	untie
7. The workers will ___ the truck at the dock.	unlock / unload / unwrap	unload
8. Are you ___ because you lost the game?	unselfish / unwilling / unhappy	unhappy

---

95

Reteaching

Sorting Using the prepared word cards from the previous game, have the child match each word containing a prefix with its definition. After the child has made the matches, have the child separate the word cards containing words with prefixes, sorting these words into three piles—one for each prefix. Once the word cards are sorted, you might encourage the child to read the word cards to you, explaining the meaning of each word.

Prefix: DIS | 151

The word disagree is dis + agree. Dis is a prefix, and agree is the base word. Circle the prefix of each word below. Underline the base word.

disappear	displease	disorder
dislike	disappoint	disagree
dishonest	dismount	disgrace

Read the words that are part of each sentence. Then circle the word that will finish the sentence. Print the word on the line.

1. When bubbles pop, you say that they _____ .	disappear / disturb / distant	disappear
2. When you do not like a thing, you say you _____ it.	disturb / dislike / discuss	dislike
3. Try to be quiet so that you will not _____ the baby.	disturb / disabled / disputed	disturb
4. If our desks are not neat, we say that they are in _____.	dismiss / dispute / disorder	disorder
5. If you do something mean, it will _____ someone.	disappear / disinfect / displease	displease
6. If Bob and Joan do not agree, we say they _____.	disagree / disappear / disorder	disagree
7. At the end of your ride on a horse, you must _____ .	disloyal / disagree / dismount	dismount
8. When you throw something away, you _____ it.	discuss / dishonest / discard	discard

---

152 | **Prefixes: RE, UN, DIS**

In each sentence, one of the prefixes in the box can be added to the word following the blank space. Read the sentence. Circle the prefix that will make sense, and write it in the space.

1. Today we will __re__ read the story that we read last week.	re / un
2. Do you __dis__ like playing marbles?	un / dis
3. It is __un__ like Ted to tell a lie.	un / dis
4. Now, __re__ write your letter on good paper.	re / un
5. Can you __un__ screw this jar lid?	dis / un
6. Please __un__ hook the screen door for your sister.	dis / un
7. The teacher will __dis__ miss the class at noon.	dis / re
8. Theresa will __re__ load the camera with film.	dis / re
9. Remember to __re__ pay the money that Dave loaned you.	un / re
10. It is __un__ fair to expect me to do all of the cleaning.	un / re
11. Did you __un__ lock the door?	un / dis

96

Unit 13 Synonyms, Antonyms, and Homonyms

Lesson 62
Synonyms (pages 153–154)

Objective The child will identify words having similar meanings as synonyms.

Review

Reading To practice recognition of prefixes and suffixes, write the following words on the chalkboard in a column: *dislike, unhappy, reread, fearful, hopeless*. Have a different child read each word and underline the base word. Then challenge the child to explain the word, including the meaning of the prefix or suffix, for example: dislike *means that something is not liked*.

Teaching Ideas

Matching Use the words above to develop the concept of synonyms. Remind the children that we often explain the meaning of a word by using a different word that means almost the same. Write these words on the chalkboard in a second column: *hate, sad, dirty, sick*. After you have written each word, challenge a volunteer to read the word and then find a word from the review list that has almost the same meaning. Have the child draw a line from the new word to the word from the review list.

Explain that when words have the same—or almost the same—meaning, they are called *synonyms*. Since the word may be unfamiliar, write it out. To help the children remember the term, you might print both *synonym* and *same* on the chalkboard, circling the two *s*'s at the beginning of each. Suggest the children use the *s*'s as a clue for remembering that *synonym* means *same* or *almost the same*.

Match-It Game Distribute the following word cards to the children: *big, close, fast, hurt, jolly, speak, steal*. Then place the following word cards on the chalkboard ledge: *happy, large, quick, harm, shut, rob, say*. Have each child find a synonym for the word he or she is holding.

Speaking To provide additional practice, use word cards or picture flashcards for the following words: *bag, bunny, bug, big, little, quick, happy, mitt*. For each word, challenge the children to think of another word that means the same or almost the same. To provide guidance to a child who has trouble thinking of a synonym, consider offering clues that use consonant sounds. For example, *What is a word for* bag *that begins with* s *and ends with* k? (sack) Compliment children who offer more than one synonym for a word.

Synonyms 153

Draw a line joining the words in each box that have the same meaning or almost the same meaning.

1. bag—sack, large—beg, happy—glad, ask—big

2. quick—fast, tardy—late, sharp—keen, rule—law

3. every—each, scowl—frown, present—gift, help—aid

4. strike—hit, poke—jab, moist—damp, spoil—rot

5. sick—ill, damage—hurt, crawl—creep, little—small

6. jump—leap, quit—stop, drop—fall, quick—fast

7. auto—car, look—see, allow—let, faint—dim

8. blend—mix, mow—cut, tidy—neat, penny—cent

9. choose—pick, price—cost, remain—stay, speak—say

10. slip—slide, total—sum, bashful—shy, simple—easy

11. plaything—toy, sport—fun, quiet—still, middle—center

12. blaze—flame, connect—join, follow—trail, distant—far

Synonyms 154

Print s on the line beside each pair of words that has the same meaning.

1. quick / fast	S	2. unhappy / sad	S	3. little / big	
4. auto / car	S	5. dry / wet		6. present / gift	S
7. look / hide		8. crawl / creep	S	9. plaything / toy	S
10. slide / slip	S	11. blend / penny		12. near / far	
13. pick / speak		14. sick / ill	S	15. tardy / late	S

Read each word. Then write another word that has the same meaning on the line.

1. large	big	2. tardy	late
3. quit	stop	4. ill	sick
5. quick	fast	6. auto	car
7. tidy	neat	8. choose	pick
9. allow	let	10. distant	far

97

Lesson 63

Antonyms (pages 155–156)

Objective   The child will identify words having opposite meanings as antonyms.

Review

Almost-Echo Game   To provide additional practice in using synonyms, write adjectives such as the following on the chalkboard: *happy, huge, wrong, dirty, fast*. Point to one of the words and then make up a sentence using that word. Then challenge a child to "almost echo" your sentence by repeating the sentence but using a synonym in place of the key word that you used, for example: *I caught a really* huge *fish yesterday* might be almost echoed as *I caught a really* big *fish yesterday*. When a child responds correctly, invite the child to make up a sentence using another word from the chalkboard and to choose a classmate to "almost echo." Praise children when more than one synonym is suggested. For example, *large, gigantic, enormous,* or *jumbo* are all common synonyms the children may know for *huge*. Consider recording synonyms the child uses under each key word. (Save these words for the Teaching Ideas activities.)

Teaching Ideas

Explain that words having opposite or almost opposite meanings are called *antonyms*. You might invite volunteers to suggest words that mean the opposite of each of the words or word groups in the Review activity.

Since the children are likely to have some difficulty distinguishing the terms *antonym* and *synonym*, write *synonym* and *same* and *antonym* and *opposite* and circle the first letter in each word. Point out that the two words that begin with different letters refer to words that have very different meanings while the words beginning with the same letter refer to words that mean the same or almost the same.

I-Disagree Game   To help children experience the concept of antonyms, consider changing the Almost-Echo Game to the I-Disagree Game. This time, for each word on the chalkboard, have the second person repeat the sentence, replacing the key word with an antonym instead of a synonym. For example, instead of almost echoing the sentence for the word *huge*, the child would say, *I disagree. I caught a really little fish yesterday*. Again, you may want to let the children know that a word may have more than one antonym just as it may have more than one synonym. For example, not only *little* but also *tiny, small,* and *itsy-bitsy* are all antonyms of *huge*.

Speaking   Display the following word cards: *bad, down, go, large, late, no, short, true*. For each, ask a child to read the word and then to give an antonym.

Antonyms   155

Draw a line joining the words in each box that have opposite meanings.

156   **Antonyms**

Print A on the line beside each pair of words with opposite meanings.

Read each word. Then write on the line another word that has the opposite meaning.

Lesson 64

Homonyms   (pages 157–160)

Objective   The child will identify words that sound alike but have different meanings and different spellings as homonyms.

Review

Are-You-an-Antonym-or-a-Synonym? Game   Use this activity to help the children differentiate between antonyms and synonyms. On the chalkboard, write the headings *Antonyms* and *Synonyms*. Then distribute word cards on which you have written pairs of words such as the following: *low/high, mend/fix, kind/nice, early/late, short/tall, glad/happy, fresh/stale, yes/no, large/big.*

Invite a volunteer to read aloud each word pair and to identify the pair as antonyms or synonyms. Have the child print the two words under the proper heading on the chalkboard.

Teaching Ideas

Listening   Direct the children to listen carefully as you say two sentences such as: *Peter ate* meat *for lunch. Josh wanted to* meet *Bob at three o'clock.* Repeat the first sentence, asking which word means *a kind of food.* Then repeat the second sentence and ask if *meet* means a kind of food in this

sentence. Ask a volunteer to give the meaning of the second word. Write the two sentences on the chalkboard, and have a volunteer circle the two words that sound alike but are spelled differently and are different in meaning. Explain that when two or more words sound alike but are different in meaning and in spelling, they are called *homonyms*. You may want to write the term for the children to see.

Speaking   Continue by writing the following sets of homonyms on the chalkboard: *be/bee, to/too/two, blue/blew, sun/son, knows/nose.* For each, ask a child to read the two words aloud and to identify the difference in spelling. Then challenge the child to explain the difference in meaning between the two words. Consider providing a definition and having the child identify which spelling goes with it. For example: *Which of the following means "a little insect that makes honey"? Is it* be *or* bee?

Writing   Write the following words and incomplete sentences on the chalkboard.

1. *You _____ girls can go to the show, _____ .*   to, too, two
2. *Gum costs only one _____ .*   sent, cent
3. *Don _____ his bike down the _____ .*   road, rode
4. *Dad _____ Brett had a _____ coat.*   knew, new
5. *Last _____ , he felt very _____ and sick.*   week, weak

99

For each, call on a child to write the correct homonym in the space. Then have the child read the completed sentence.

Extension

Reading/Writing   You might refer to the classroom collection or to the library for one of the amusing picture books on homonyms such as Fred Gwynne's *The King That Rained*. Give the child an opportunity to enjoy the words and pictures. Consider challenging the child to use the book as a model for writing sentences in which the wrong homonym is used. Some of the best silly homonym sentences might be illustrated and collected for a classroom book.

Family Involvement Activity   Duplicate the Family Letter on page 109 of this Teacher's Edition. Send it home with the children.

Homonyms 159

Read the words that are part of each sentence. Then circle the word in the box that will finish the sentence. Print the word on the line.

1. We may see a __deer__ while we are camping.	deer / dear
2. Do you think that we will __see__ a fox, too?	sea / **see**
3. June can catch fish in this brook with her rod and __reel__.	real / **reel**
4. May we eat our meals __here__ under this tree?	hear / **here**
5. Kim __heard__ some people talking in the next room.	**heard** / herd
6. Ted __knew__ how to swim when he was three.	**knew** / new
7. The cave seems dark after being in the __sun__.	son / **sun**
8. "Let's wait until next __week__ to explore it," said Dad.	**week** / weak
9. Linda knows how to swim and dive well, __too__.	**too** / to
10. How much is the bus __fare__ to town?	fair / **fare**
11. We enjoyed telling tall __tales__ about the old West.	tails / **tales**

---

160   Crossword Puzzle Review

Fill in the crossword puzzle. The sounds you learned in this book will help you. Look at the clues in parentheses. The first one has been done for you.

Across
1. hangs on a branch (ea spells long e)
3. has the same meaning as penny (soft sound of c)
5. large bird (s blend)
7. touch gently (short a)
8. has the same meaning as eat (long i)
9. dogs and cats (short e)
11. places to sleep (short e)
13. what we hear with
14. helps get things clean (long o)
15. home of birds (s blend on the end)

Down
2. the suffix used to form the plural of dish
3. a kind of heavy string (hard c)
4. something in the woods (long e)
5. a synonym for stain
6. it flies in the wind (long i)
9. things used to write and draw (short e)
10. take one giant _____ (s blend)
11. your birthday celebrates the day you were _____
12. opposite of hard

100

Date: _____

A Note to the Family—

We are using PHONICS IS FUN in your child's class. The skills taught in the program will help your child become a better reader. I will send a Family Involvement Activity home with your child for most phonics units. These activities are similar to those your child _____ does in school. Your participation in these activities will help your child develop and review the skills learned in the classroom.

The following Family Involvement Activity reviews the skills covered in Unit Two. This activity involves little preparation, and the materials are common household items. For the Unit Two activity, your child will list the names of objects that begin with the consonant letters $b, c, d, f, g, h, j, k, l, m, n, p, q(u), r, s, t, v, w, x, y,$ and z.

Have your child write the consonant letters of the alphabet in a column down the left side of a sheet of paper. Then accompany your child through your neighborhood on a Beginning Consonant Scavenger Hunt. (You might conduct the hunt in places such as stores, parks, and yards.) Encourage your child to look for objects with names that begin with the consonant letters of the alphabet. Help your child write the name of each object next to the appropriate letter on the paper. For the letter x, you may wish to have your child list the name of an object that ends with that consonant sound. Additionally, the letter z may present a special challenge.

Please encourage your child to complete this activity at home with the family's assistance. Completed pages may be returned to the classroom by (date) _____ and will become part of our classroom materials.

Thank you for your cooperation. Your comments are always welcome.

Sincerely,

Comments: _____

Date: _____

A Note to the Family—

We are using PHONICS IS FUN in your child's class. The skills taught in the program will help your child become a better reader. I will send a Family Involvement Activity home with your child for most phonics units. These activities are similar to those your child _____ does in school. Your participation in these activities will help your child develop and review the skills learned in the classroom.

The following Family Involvement Activity reviews the skills covered in Unit Four. This activity involves little preparation, and the materials are common household items. For the Unit Four activity, your child will write the names of objects that have the long sounds of the vowels *a, e, i, o,* and *u.*

Have your child write the following headings in a row on a sheet of paper: *Long a, Long e, Long i, Long o, Long u.* Then accompany your child on a trip to look for objects with names that have these vowel sounds. Encourage your child to look for objects while walking or riding on the bus, in the car, or on the train. You might suggest that your child write the names of objects as they are seen, listing as many words for each long vowel sound as possible. Encourage your child not to worry about spelling at this first stage. Later, help your child correct misspelled words. Ask your child to recopy the work on a clean sheet of paper, entitling the paper *Long Vowel Guide.*

Please help your child prepare this *Long Vowel Guide* at home with your family's assistance. Completed guides may be returned to the classroom by (date) _____ and will become part of our classroom display.

Thank you for your cooperation. Your comments are always welcome.

Sincerely,

Comments: _____

_____

_____

_____

_____

_____

Date: _____

A Note to the Family—

We are using PHONICS IS FUN in your child's class. The skills taught in the program
will help your child become a better reader. I will send a Family Involvement Activity
home with your child for most phonics units. These activities are similar to those your
child _____ does in school. Your participation in these activities
will help your child develop and review the skills learned in the classroom.

The following Family Involvement Activity reviews the skills covered in Unit Six. This
activity involves little preparation, and the materials are common household items. For
the Unit Six activity, your child will sort word cards into the following groups: those
containing words with the soft sound of c *(face)*, those containing words with the hard
sound of c *(can)*, those containing words with the soft sound of g *(page)*, and those
containing words with the hard sound of g *(wig)*.

Provide index cards or small squares of cardboard or paper. Help your child prepare
word cards by writing words that have the hard or soft sounds of c and g. You might
suggest the following words: *fence, cap, cup, pencil, cake, mice, camel, celery, face,
wage, huge, gem, giant, good, gave, goat, game, dog*. Encourage your child to suggest
additional words that have these sounds. Shuffle the word cards, and then challenge your
child to sort them by sound in groups for *hard c, soft c, hard g,* and *soft g*.

Please help your child fasten each group of cards with a rubber band, labeling each as
soft or hard c or g sounds. Completed cards may be returned to the classroom by
(date) _____ and will become part of our classroom display.

Thank you for your cooperation. Your comments are always welcome.

Sincerely,

Comments: _____
_____
_____
_____
_____
_____
_____

Date: _____

A Note to the Family—

We are using PHONICS IS FUN in your child's class. The skills taught in the program will help your child become a better reader. I will send a Family Involvement Activity home with your child for most phonics units. These activities are similar to those your child _____ does in school. Your participation in these activities will help your child develop and review the skills learned in the classroom.

The following Family Involvement Activity reviews the skills covered in Unit Eight. This activity involves little preparation, and the materials are common household items. For the Unit Eight activity, your child will play a game, matching contractions with the phrases they stand for. (Your child will know that a *contraction* is a short way of combining two words with an apostrophe, such as *don't* for *do not*.)

Play a game of Go Fish in which both players try to match contractions with the phrases they stand for. Prepare the game materials by helping your child write each of the following phrases and contractions on index cards or squares of cardboard.

I will	*I'll*	*you will*	*you'll*
I am	*I'm*	*we will*	*we'll*
is not	*isn't*	*do not*	*don't*
it is	*it's*	*they are*	*they're*
let us	*let's*	*we have*	*we've*
he will	*he'll*	*she is*	*she's*

Shuffle the cards and deal five cards to your child and five to yourself. Keep the remaining cards in a stack on the table. Take turns asking each other for the phrase or contraction that "matches" a card being held. For example, the word card *do not* matches the word card *don't*. If a player cannot receive a matching card from the other player, that person may "fish" for the card by drawing a card from the stack on the table. The winner is the person with the most matches when all the cards from the stack have been drawn.

Please help your child write each of the phrases and contractions used in the game on a sheet of paper. Completed lists of phrases and contractions may be returned to the classroom by (date) _____ and will become part of our classroom display.

Thank you for your cooperation. Your comments are always welcome.

Sincerely,

Comments: _____

_____

_____

Date: _____

A Note to the Family—

We are using PHONICS IS FUN in your child's class. The skills taught in the program will help your child become a better reader. I will send a Family Involvement Activity home with your child for most phonics units. These activities are similar to those your child _____ does in school. Your participation in these activities will help your child develop and review the skills learned in the classroom.

The following Family Involvement Activity reviews the skills covered in Unit Nine. This activity involves little preparation, and the materials are common household items. For the Unit Nine activity, your child will identify words that have the same vowel digraph. (Your child will know that a *vowel digraph* is a double vowel that does not follow the usual phonetic rule for long vowels. Let the words *moon, book, head, paw,* and *auto* serve as guides.)

Play the following card game to give your child practice at finding words with the same vowel digraph. Help your child write the following words on index cards or on squares of cardboard: *food, coop, room, boot, look, wood, book, foot, head, thread, head, read, bread, pawn, paw, saucer, auto, raw, saw, because, faucet.* Shuffle the word cards and place them facedown in a stack on the table. Take turns with your child, choosing two cards from the stack, and reading the words to determine whether the words have the same digraph. If the word cards have the same digraph, the player keeps both word cards. If the digraphs in the two word cards do not match, both cards should be placed faceup on the table. On subsequent turns, the players may either draw two word cards from the stack, or they may match the first card drawn with one that is faceup on the table. The player with the most pairs at the end of the game is the winner.

Please encourage your child to list each word pair found in the game. Completed lists of word pairs may be returned to the classroom by (date) _____ and will become part of our classroom materials.

Thank you for your cooperation. Your comments are always welcome.

Sincerely,

Comments: _____

_____

_____

_____

Date: _____

A Note to the Family—

We are using PHONICS IS FUN in your child's class. The skills taught in the program
will help your child become a better reader. I will send a Family Involvement Activity
home with your child for most phonics units. These activities are similar to those your
child _____ does in school. Your participation in these activities
will help your child develop and review the skills learned in the classroom.

The following Family Involvement Activity reviews the skills covered in Unit Thirteen.
This activity involves little preparation, and the materials are common household items.
For the Unit Thirteen activity, your child will identify synonyms, antonyms, and
homonyms for common words. (Your child will know that *synonyms* are words having
similar meanings, such as *bag/sack; antonyms* are words having opposite meanings, such
as *yes/no;* and *homonyms* are words having the same pronunciation, but different
meanings and spellings, such as *sail/sale.*)

Write the following words in a column down the left side of a sheet of paper: *night,
peak, male, tale, pale, prince, right, sea.* Then write the following headings in a row
across the top of the paper: *Synonyms, Antonyms, Homonyms.* Challenge your child to
think of either a synonym, an antonym, or a homonym for each of the words on the page.
Help your child write these words in the appropriate space on the paper. Encourage your
child to think of words for the other categories.

Please encourage your child to complete the page at home with your family's assistance.
Completed pages may be returned to the classroom by (date) _____ and will
become part of our classroom materials.

Thank you for your cooperation. Your comments are always welcome.

Sincerely,

Comments: _____
_____
_____
_____
_____
_____

Phonics Is Fun
Index of Skills

	Lesson Numbers		
	Book 1	Book 2	Book 3
Antonyms		63	60
Compound words			
long vowel		23	14
short vowel		16	10
Consonants			
digraphs	66–68	29, 30, 58, 59	18, 19, 34, 35
hard and soft *c*		31	21, 23
hard and soft *g*		32	22, 23
l blends	63	25	16
letter-sound association	8–27	2–10	2–4
r blends	62	24	15
s blends	64	26	17
Contractions		46–49	58
Ending *le*		60	36
Homonyms		64	61
Prefixes		61	46–49
Recognition of letters	2–7	1	1
Suffixes	59–61	36–45	39–44, 57
Syllabication			37, 38, 45, 50–56
Synonyms		62	59
Two-syllable words		17, 23	10
Visual discrimination	1		
Vowels			
digraphs		50–53	27–30
diphthongs		54–57	31–33
long *a*	43–45	18	11
long *e*	55–57	22	13
long *i*	46–48	19	11
long *o*	52–54	21	12
long *u*	49–51	20	12
review of	58		
seen and heard			37
short *a*	28–30	11	5
short *e*	40–42	15	9
short *i*	31–33	12	6
short *o*	37–39	14	8
short *u*	34–36	13	7
w		28	20
with *r*		33–35	24–26
y	65	27	20

Made in the USA
Columbia, SC
01 September 2020

17079544R00061